The
STUDENT
TEACHER'S
HANDBOOK

The STUDENT TEACHER'S HANDBOOK

CHRISTINE EDWARDS & MAURA HEALY

KOGAN
PAGE

First published in 1994

Kogan Page Limited
120 Page Limited Road
London N1 9JN

British Library Cataloguing in Publication Data

A CIP record for this book is available from the British Library.

ISBN 0 7494 1371 9

Typeset by Saxon Graphics Ltd, Derby
Printed and bound in Great Britain by Clays Ltd, St Ives plc

Contents

Introduction

Our book has been written to support you in the exciting and challenging process of becoming a teacher. You have chosen to enter the profession at a time of increasing change in schools and in the curriculum. Teacher training courses are also part of this change. You and your fellow students will be following courses which are significantly different from those followed by students before 1993. You will notice that your tutors at your Higher Education Institution (HEI) and in the schools in which you teach are very aware of this change and that they will still be adjusting to the change. You will have less adjustment to make. So much of what you do will be new that you will not be unduly concerned about 'how we used to do it in the old days'.

However, you will find that the course may differ in many respects from courses you have undertaken in the past.

'At first I found the competences daunting but they made me realise that I was entering a profession.'

This is how one student finishing his PGCE at Leeds University described his experience of one key feature of the course. You are assessed against an explicit list of *competences* published by the Department for Education (DFE). Appendix 1 gives this list. Your HEI, in partnership with schools, may well have devised its own version of these competences. What may be new for you is that you have to *prove* during your course that you can *demonstrate* that you are competent in all these areas. Essentially you need to provide evidence that you can teach:

- these pupils in this school
- in these curriculum areas
- to a specific standard of competence.

You are expected to be active in this process. This means that you must collect evidence of your competence and you must demonstrate that you are able to reflect on your learning and to action plan for further learning. This book helps you in this process.

■ We take you through the significant phases in your learning about teaching.

■ We help you to make sense of your learning, and to identify and build evidence of that learning.

■ We help you to take an active part in planning and managing your own learning.

PHASES IN LEARNING ABOUT TEACHING

This book helps you work through and reflect on the different phases of your learning about teaching.

Chapter 1 helps you:

■ make sense of all the information that comes to you in a new course or a new school

■ find out more about the school(s) in which you will be learning to teach

■ find ways of working with all the people who are available to help you

■ begin to prepare yourself for the ways in which you will be assessed.

Chapter 2 supports you as you begin to take increasing responsibility for your own classes. Initially you might share this task with 'host teachers'. These are the teachers who regularly teach the groups to which you have been allocated.

This way of working in called 'collaborative teaching'.

Chapter 3 focuses on solo teaching. This chapter helps you extend your skills to meet the demands that arise when you are expected to teach a whole class for one whole lesson and to design a scheme of work which will meet the needs of all the pupils for whom you are responsible.

Chapter 4 helps you manage the process of:

■ assessing and recording the learning of your pupils in the programme you have taught

■ sharing the assessment with pupils, teachers and parents

■ identifying your learning and prioritising future targets for yourself

■ managing your time to meet the targets and deadlines occurring towards the end of your time in a particular school.

Chapter 5 has a slightly different emphasis. It looks forward to your future career and helps you:

■ identify where you would like to work and the kinds of schools in which you would like to work

■ present yourself well to future employers

■ prepare for a new job and think ahead for your further professional development.

MAKING SENSE OF YOUR LEARNING

It is important to be aware of your own learning needs, to plan for future learning and to record successes and new targets. Each chapter supports you in this process. They all have a similar format. Each one includes:

■ *an introduction* to what we hope you will learn

■ help on *getting started* in each of the phases we consider

■ strategies for *making the most of your opportunities* in each phase of your learning

■ strategies for *handling any difficult situations* which might arise

- help in *preparing for your own assessment*
- help in *looking forward* to the next phase of your learning.

Each chapter encourages you to undertake a range of tasks which together will enable you to:

- demonstrate your competences in all the areas identified by the Department for Education
- take an active role in identifying and planning to meet your learning needs.

BUILDING FOR THE FUTURE

Your initial teacher training is only the start of what will be a career-long process of learning. Our book aims to help you develop the habit of critically reviewing your growing competence and an ability to continue to plan for and resource future learning. The best teachers are those who are open to opportunities for further professional development.

Induction

INTRODUCTION

At the start of your initial teacher training course there will undoubtedly be a lot of information to absorb as well as a new environment to get used to. There will be new people with whom you will be working. Both the way you will be expected to learn and the way you will be assessed may be very different from your previous experience.

It is important to make a good start. There are things you need to do if you are to find your feet quickly. You need to feel confident and able to learn in what may initially feel a rather bewildering environment.

The purpose of this chapter is to help you make the best of your induction by:

■ helping you draw a map of:

  – your year in training
  – your course and its components
  – the support structures available to you
  – your course requirements

■ helping you to understand and begin to use a new model for your assessment. This has to be based on a list of competences you will need to acquire and demonstrate

■ helping you find ways of working with key people

- helping you find new ways of learning for yourself and by yourself
- smoothing your path into the next stage of your course when you will begin to teach.

This chapter invites you to undertake activities in which you will:

- **begin to acquire new skills** for learning which will be essential for your course. You will need to develop skills in:
  - observing and reflecting on the teaching you have seen or in which you have played a part. This will need to become second nature to you
  - reading. You will need to read and assimilate a very wide range of material
  - managing your time in new ways. You will find much of your time is already accounted for by the programme of your course – all the more reason to plan carefully the time over which you have control, as there is a great deal to be done
  - negotiating ways of working productively with others. A lot of what you will need to learn will come from teachers in school, HEI tutors and lecturers and other students
  - reflecting on the scope and quality of your learning. You will need to take responsibility for collecting, and getting validated, appropriate evidence of your growing competence

- **develop new ways of thinking** about your subject – there is a world of difference between a literary critic or Kenneth Branagh and a Year 9 pupil encountering Shakespeare for the first time. You will need to bridge that gap, match the National Curriculum demands and understand the place of your subject in the school curriculum

- **begin to explore how lessons work** – how they are planned, how teachers organise and promote learning

- **get to grips with your course** – its structure, its assessment requirements, the deadlines you must meet and, most importantly, how to utilise the support available to you in HEI and school

■ **find out more about your schools** and their communities.

MAPPING YOUR LEARNING

The learning you do in this chapter and at the beginning of your course will be of great value throughout your course. It is worthwhile reflecting on this as you go along and keeping track of your learning. Take time to think about:

■ the skills you are using and developing, especially those which are new or less familiar to you, eg, action planning your own learning activities

■ aspects of teaching and of the subjects in the school curriculum. Do they fit your expectations? What are you learning about the 'language' of teaching?

■ what you are discovering about pupils, about how they learn and about teaching strategies.

GETTING STARTED

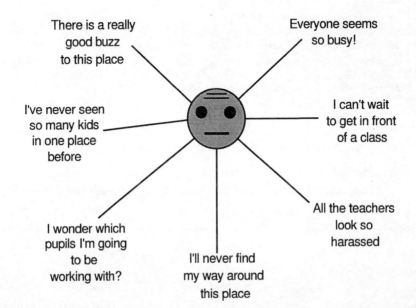

When you begin, it will probably seem that there is so much that is new and so much to learn that you do not know how or where to get started. You are likely to be wondering how you can get to grips with all the information that is flying your way, wondering what the course is really about, what is really important and what it is that you need to do first. Perhaps that is why you have bought this book!

Some helpful ways to get a good start are:

- **by being a reflective learner;** you will need to keep a log and spend time thinking about the questions and issues which emerge day-to-day. Your log will help you see patterns developing over time

- **by building on your strengths** and enthusiasm. Know what they are and where they might be useful in the challenges you face

- **by keeping track of what is going on** – in the course, in your schools, with other students

- **by understanding** and providing for your own learning needs.

A log enables you to:

- record and reflect on insights and questions arising from your experiences

- collect evidence of your thinking. This evidence will be of use in your own assessment

- impose your own order on the disparate and extensive range of experience and information which your course will generate

- learn from patterns that emerge over time

- plan for your further learning by building a picture of your developing competence and identifying new targets.

Your HEI may recommend a particular format for a log; they may even give it a different name such as a diary, a journal, or a portfolio. The important thing is to capture significant impressions, ideas and information while they are still fresh, so that you do not lose them and can reflect on them objectively when you have a better perspective and more time.

When you set up a log you will need to organise it in such a way as to achieve maximum flexibility, for example, a loose-leaf A4 binder with dividers.

Task 1: Getting Ready for Learning

■ What aspects of your course are you looking forward to? Make a list of these in your log. Why you are looking forward to them? Check out when and how opportunities for these will be available to you.

■ Some things you need to know as early as possible, if you are going to manage your time efficiently, are:

- who is responsible for you in each of the institutions where you will be working?
- when will you be in each of these places?
- when will you be teaching your first class?
- how and when are you assessed?
- who will be your particular mentor(s) or closest support?
- what feedback will you get about your work? When and how will you get it?
- what deadlines do you have to meet?
- what private study time do you have?

You can probably think of more questions. Do you know the answers? If not, who are you going to get to answer them for you? Decide when and where you are going to get them answered. Make a note in your log.

When you learn to teach you will need to be able to learn in many different ways. Figure 1.1 is a 'map' of some strategies you will need to be able to use.

Figure 1.1 *Learning to Teach*

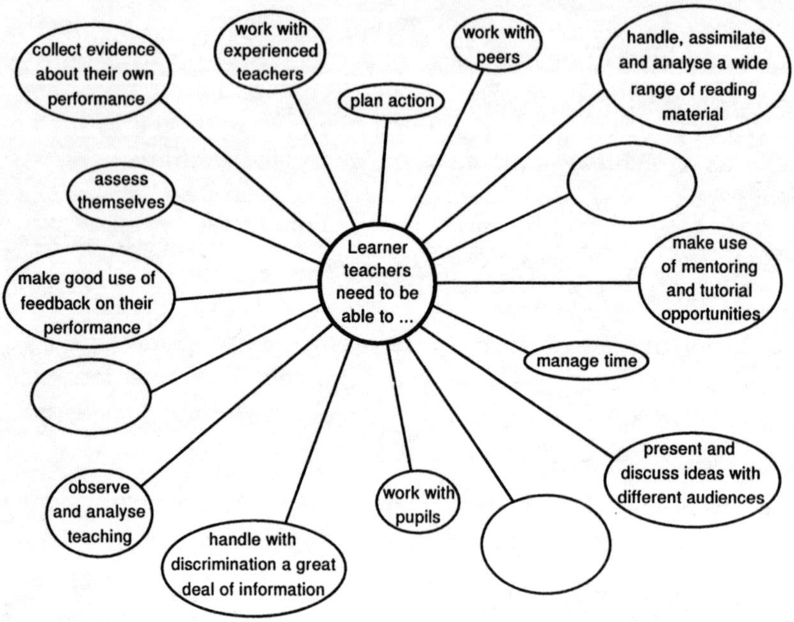

Task 2: Learning How to Learn

You will see that there are some empty bubbles in Figure 1.1.

- Fill in these with ideas of your own. What else do you think learner teachers on a course like yours will need to be able to do?

- Choose two or three bubbles, ours or yours, and think about how you might further develop these skills in yourself.

- Consider when, where and with whom you will work on these skills.

MAKING THE MOST OF YOUR OPPORTUNITIES
MAKING THE MOST OF YOUR SCHOOL

When you begin to work in a school you can expect to get a lot of new information. Figure 1.2 offers you some guidance on the information you might expect to receive.

Figure 1.2 *Finding out about your school*

The school might give you the following information:	Find out for yourself by:
maps - plan of buildings - local map	■ compiling a scrapbook about the school and the communities it serves. Use: – newspaper articles – school magazines – photographs – quotes from pupils you talk to
pupil, staff and parent handbooks	
calendar of events	
	■ being a fly on the wall: – eat lunch with the children – spend time on the corridors – talk to people in the staff room and school office
list of staff names and responsibilities	
key policy documents, including pupil behaviour code	■ finding out which meetings you can attend and going to as many as possible (including governors' meetings)
details of people with whom you will be working most closely and of the programme you will be following together	■ finding out about parent-teacher activities; join in where you can
	■ observing pupils on their way to and from school, in local shops and on public transport

---

Task 3: Noting First Impressions

■ Review the information you have acquired about your school.

■ Think of five words or phrases that describe your school from the point of view of a teacher. Justify your choice with evidence and examples.

■ Now do the same thing from the point of view of a pupil.

■ Put your reflections into your log.

MAKING THE MOST OF YOUR OBSERVATIONS

The task you have just done will help you reflect on the 'feel' of your school; now focus on classrooms. You can learn about what happens in classrooms by observing:

- specific pupils for a day or more
- a whole class over a period of time
- a sub-group of pupils (eg, very able girls) in different contexts
- a teacher with contrasting groups
- a group at different times of the day
- a subject which differs from your own.

CASE STUDY 1

Arif and Ruth are newly arrived student-teachers in the same school. They have been given the opportunity to observe one class's experience of a sequence of three science lessons and to interview the teacher at the end. Their tutor has given them some questions to help them make the best of this learning opportunity. The following is an extract from their notes made during this tutorial.

What do you want to look at?

> managing health and safety *X*

> giving out equipment *X*

> use of question and answer *X*

> difference in experiences of boys and girls ✓ – A

> groupwork ✓ – B

How are you going to make sure you see what you want to see?

> focus on one group for a period of time

> prepare in advance specific questions about the group

> plan to sit outside the group where I can see everybody

> explain that I just want to see how they learn and that they should just get on normally

How will you record what you see and hear?

For A: Arif will keep a note of the number and type of questions the teacher addresses to girls and to boys.

Ruth will make notes of the things they say using a format we have designed in advance, so that she can just tick a category to indicate kinds of contributions the girls make and the ways the boys in the group respond to them.

For B: We will tape-record the group and analyse how they share tasks and ideas.

How will you make use of the record you have collected?

For A and B: meet immediately after each lesson and discuss what we have observed, looking for:

> areas where our different forms of evidence agree or conflict

> whether our evidence confirms or contradicts our expectations

> areas to explore in discussion with the teacher
> ways we will present our observations to the teacher

ways in which we might adjust the focus and strategy for our observations next time

What questions will you want to ask the teacher?

For A: Was what we observed typical of the class?

How far is the class typical of other classes?

What was the teacher trying to achieve, especially in terms of the involvement of boys and girls?

What were the problems she felt she faced?

What strategies, other than the ones we observed, could she tell us about?

Your HEI tutor will probably provide you with ideas for other approaches.

Task 4: Learning from Observations

You will be given observation opportunities similar to those made available to Ruth and Arif.

■ Check how many lessons you will be able to observe and whether you will be able to discuss your observations with the teachers involved.

■ Negotiate with the teachers possible focuses for your observations and the time they will allocate to subsequent discussions.

■ Use the questions which were the starting point for Ruth and Arif to structure your own preparation. Check out your proposals with the teachers concerned.

■ Choose the best strategies to:

  – access the information you want
  – record it
  – analyse and present it for discussion with fellow students or the teacher.

MAKING THE MOST OF YOUR MENTOR

In *Getting Started* you found out who your mentors are and how often you can expect to meet with them. If you don't know this yet, make sure you find out.

Mentors:

- are your first line of support
- know you well and meet you regularly
- help you plan your learning purposefully
- invite you into their classrooms and share their teaching with you
- observe your lessons and give you feedback and support
- play a crucial role in your assessment
- work closely with your HEI in planning and delivering your course.

You will probably find that time for meetings and discussion with your mentor, or anyone else, is at a premium. You must be well organised if you are to get the best out of the meetings available to you. Whenever you arrange a meeting make sure you:

- **clarify** when, where and for how long you will meet
  what the meeting will be about
  what you need to bring and what you want your mentor to bring
  what you are going to say, ask, or decide by negotiation
- **prepare** the papers you need:
  - observations and evidence
  - notes of issues for further discussion.

Good meetings are:

- planned
- prepared
- open
- based on evidence.

They work best when all parties are open to feedback.

You will meet regularly with your mentor and you will increasingly rely on her/him to give you feedback about your teaching. At this early stage, you need to establish ways of working together which will be helpful and creative. It is important to think about what you contribute to this professional relationship and to seek to improve your skills in learning collaboratively with other adults.

Task 5: Building a Professional Dialogue

Imagine you are a fly on the wall of a meeting with your mentor. In what ways do you help or hinder the process of professional dialogue?

- Draw up a grid like the one in Figure 1.3. Think about what
    - was provided and received
    - was heard and said
    - was proposed and agreed
    - helped and hindered the process.

    Make notes about your contribution and that of your mentor in respect of each category.

- Decide upon two specific things you would do differently next time.

Figure 1.3 *Making the most of meetings*

provided	received
I brought my observation notes of her lesson. She brought her lesson plan.	She gave me a couple of pupils' books to look at. She made me aware of the difficulties of keeping groups on task.
heard	**said**
We talked a lot about different pupils' needs. I got lots of ideas.	I asked a lot of questions about pupils. She explained how the lesson had been adjusted for the most able and the least able.
proposed	**agreed**
We thought we needed to work together more in planning any future observation.	She agreed to give me lesson plans in advance next time. I agreed to propose and discuss a different observation approach with her.
helped	**hindered**
We shared written notes and plans. We identified key questionswe wanted to talk about.	I didn't know enough about the class. She thought I was being more critical than I intended.

MANAGING DIFFICULT SITUATIONS

A CRISIS OF CONFIDENCE

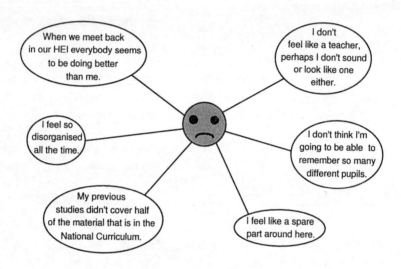

You will probaly be having one or two thoughts like these; almost everyone does. It is perfectly normal: what matters most is your ability to clarify your worries, to share them and get them in perspective.

Who should you approach? You have mentors in school and in your HEI or you might prefer to turn to others for advice or a sympathetic ear: another student-teacher, a newly qualified teacher or a senior member of staff might all be able to help with different kinds of worries. Whoever you talk to, it is important to keep your mentor in the picture. You don't have to go into details but s/he should be aware that you have had worries and have been supported.

Task 6: Managing Worries

Here are some ways of dealing with worries.

■ Think about who you would approach with your
worry and write a note asking for a chat and
explain what you want to talk about – you may not
even need to send it once it is written.

■ Make a rough list of all the worries and complaints
that come into your head.

  – Select the key points and write them on to separate slips
    of paper.
  – Pick out one at a time and consider how you
    would start a conversation about it with a
    mentor or friend. Make notes on the relevant slip.
  – Consider what response you would hope to
    get. This might be enough to solve your worry.
  – If not, review your slips of paper again and
    decide which ones you still need help with.
  – Decide with whom you would like to talk
    about them and when and where would be best.

AM I MAKING THE MOST OF THIS?

Your course has been designed to offer you:

■ specific kinds of support from the school and the HEI

■ opportunities for observation

■ opportunities for collaborative teaching

■ opportunities to teach by yourself

■ regular reviews and feedback to help you and your mentor
  map your growing competence.

Sometimes you may feel you are not getting the learning
opportunities and the support you need for your professional
development.

CASE STUDY 2

Simon's mentor is not enthusiastic about her new role. Scheduled meetings are regularly cancelled because she has 'other commitments'. Worse still, Simon is having great difficulty in deciding how to discuss the lessons he has observed because he realises his mentor's lessons are consistently unplanned and lack any real focus.

One way Simon might approach this problem is to use a SWOT (Strengths, Weaknesses, Opportunities and Threats) analysis of the situation.

He needs to ask himself:

What are the *strengths* of my situation?	eg, he is based in a good department
What are the *weaknesses*?	eg, he dare not be over-critical
What *opportunities* do I have to do something different?	eg, he can get help from his HEI tutor
What *threats* are there that could make things worse? (How might I make things worse?)	eg, if he doesn't begin to learn something soon his assessments will suffer.

The story continues

Simon decides to take action and enlists the support of his HEI tutor who, in turn, discusses the problem with the deputy head-teacher of the school. They decide that a new mentor needs to be allocated, and speedily. Within a couple of days Simon begins to work with someone who is able to give him the time he needs and whose classroom is one in which he feels comfortable.

Whether or not you have as obvious a problem as Simon's, it is worth reflecting from time to time on whether you are getting the best out of your programme.

Task 7: Keeping it Under Review

- Gather together all the *evidence* you have collected about your opportunities and experiences to date.

- In your log, *analyse and reflect* on it by doing a SWOT analysis like Simon's. Are you making the most of your opportunities?

- Commit yourself to a *plan of action* which tackles one specific weakness by building on an opportunity or a strength which you know you have.

You can use a SWOT analysis whenever you have a difficult decision to make or you feel you are not making progress in solving a problem.

PREPARING FOR ASSESSMENT

WHAT DO YOU BRING WITH YOU?

You can probably think of quite a few attributes you have which you hope are going to help you be a good teacher. You have personal skills and qualities as well as knowledge. How far have your studies really prepared you to teach in a school? You know a great deal about the subjects you have studied and have developed high-level skills. However, it is possible to know both too much and too little, for example:

	Too much	*Too little*
Content	early medieval literature	modern children's literature
Skills	how to write a 20,000 word essay	how I learned to write my first essay

---

Task 8: Your Specialisation in the School Curriculum

- Draw a grid like the one in the example above.

- Use it to consider some of the ways in which you might know 'too much' and 'too little' about the subjects you intend to teach.

- In your log, note:

  - things you could do to bridge the gap between your existing knowledge and the demands of the National Curriculum
  - ways in which you can make your existing skills and knowledge accessible to the pupils you will teach.

HOW WILL YOUR NEW LEARNING BE ASSESSED?

Your formal assessment is not a 'one-off' event at an appointed time and place where you perform for an examiner; it will be continuous and it will be based on your day-to-day practical teaching.

The Department for Education (DFE) requires you to be assessed on aspects of being a teacher called competences (see Appendix 1). To demonstrate these you will have to take responsibility for collecting and providing your assessor with evidence of your competence.

You will need to demonstrate a wide range of skills and understanding and you will need to make honest and accurate assessments of your own learning to prepare this evidence. This kind of assessment is best prepared for by an *action planning* process which we take you through in Task 9.

At this stage you have only taken the early steps in the process of preparing for assessment. This is evident when you compare yourself with the following DFE competences.

Subject knowledge

Newly-qualified teachers should be able to demonstrate:

- an understanding of the knowledge, concepts and skills of their specialist subjects and of the place of these subjects in the school curriculum;

- knowledge and understanding of the National Curriculum Attainment Targets (NCATs) and the programmes of study (PoS) in the subjects they are preparing to teach, together with an understanding of the framework of the statutory requirements;

- a breadth and depth of subject knowledge extending beyond PoS and examination syllabuses in school.

This is the first of the DFE competence areas and you will note that it relates closely to Task 8.

Task 9: Action Planning

- Choose one of the competence statements in the box above. Consider what you need to be able to do to demonstrate it:
  - what you need to learn – your *learning needs*
  - which needs you can realistically work on at this point in time – your *targets*
  - what you can do to learn the things you have set as your targets – your *action plan*
  - what evidence you will gather to help you check the progress you are making – your *review*.

CASE STUDY 3

Here is how one English student worked her way through this process.

I don't know enough about teenage fiction *(learning needs)*.

I should plan to read and review at least one novel each week *(targets)*.

I'll get advice on what to read from:

■ teachers

■ my HEI tutors

■ the school librarian

■ school pupils

■ my local bookshop

(*action plan 1*).

I'll need to check out which authors are stipulated by the examination boards and the National Curriculum (*action plan 2*).

I will build up a set of index cards in which I keep details of writers, novels and themes so I can cross-reference them for different age groups. (*review*).

This is the *action planning* process. You can use these questions whenever you are planning learning activities. Further chapters contain activities which will help you develop expertise in action planning.

DEVELOPING AN EVIDENCE BASE

Figure 1.4 gives different ways of collecting and recording the evidence you will need to persuade your assessor(s) that you are beginning to acquire the necessary competences.

Your log will be an excellent source of evidence. It will also help you to check that you are meeting the targets you have set yourself.

Figure 1.4 *Sources of evidence*

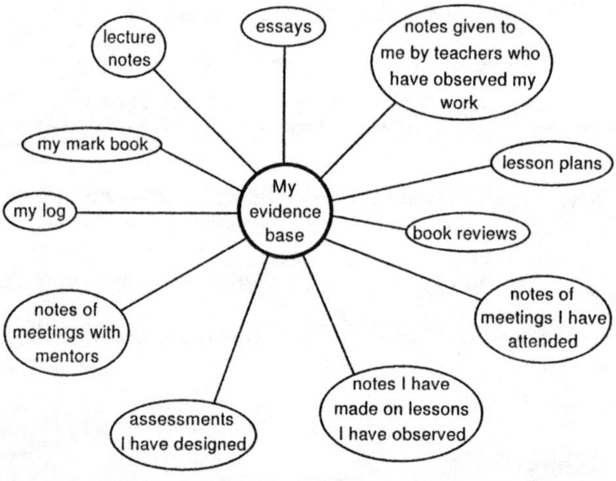

Task 10: Building Your Evidence Base

- Bring together all the evidence about your learning for the last two weeks.

- Decide what additional evidence you need to collect if you are to demonstrate your competence in the area of *subject knowledge*. Write action plans such as the one suggested in the last task. Remember your action plan also provides evidence of your learning.

- Plan how you will collect the evidence you need.

- Discuss with your mentor at school or your HEI when and how you will be able to present and discuss your evidence.

LOOKING FORWARD

As you work your way through this book, you will be able to observe your own progress in key areas of the skills and competences you are going to need as a teacher. This chapter has focused on the areas highlighted in the following chart:

Core Skills	Teaching Competences*
Action planning	*Subject Knowledge*
Problem solving	SK1
Self-assessment	SK2
record keeping	SK3
Observation	*Subject Application*
using feedback	SA3
using information	SA5
Collecting evidence	*Classroom Management*
Working with adults	
working with pupils	*Assessment and Recording*
analysis	*of Pupils' Progress*
evaluating	*Further Professional*
managing people	*Development*
time	FPD1
resources	FPD3
	FPD7

(*Appendix 1 gives full details of these competences and an explanation of the codes used.)

Task 11: Logging Your Progress

Think about the skills and competences on which this chapter focused:

■ with which have you made progress?

■ which will form new targets for you?

Use your log to make a note of your progress and of the areas you still need to work on.

The next chapter will help you prepare for working collaboratively in the classroom. You will learn how to plan, teach and evaluate a lesson.

Task 12: Thinking Ahead

■ Think about the core skills you most need to develop for this new challenge.

■ Use the *action planning* process to help you develop them.

CHAPTER 2

Learning By Teaching Collaboratively

INTRODUCTION

While you may be keen to get into classrooms and begin teaching by yourself, one of the most effective ways of learning how to teach is to plan, teach and evaluate a lesson jointly with another teacher or with another learner teacher.

This way you can share the task of generating ideas and assessing how far they meet the needs of all the pupils in the class. Classrooms are fast-moving, busy places. It's hard to make sense of them by yourself, especially at first, and you will learn a lot by enlisting a colleague to work with you to meet this challenge.

The purpose of this chapter is to help you to explore ways of working in a range of contexts so that you can learn about:

■ yourself as a learner teacher

■ the children you teach

■ how teachers can and do support each other

■ responding to different contexts; a mixed ability Year 7 is very different from a top set Year 11. You will need different strategies and different resources

> ■ making best use of the opportunities offered by your course. You will need to learn how to get help from lecturers, teachers and fellow students.

This chapter, then, will invite you to undertake activities which will:

■ extend your skills

■ challenge your ways of thinking

■ explore ways of working with teachers, fellow students and pupils

■ make sense of your first experiences

■ build up evidence about yourself as a learner teacher.

MAPPING YOUR LEARNING

As you work through this chapter and begin collaborative teaching, you need to value and record your learning. Take time to think about how far you have:

■ learned to take an increasing responsibility for the planning process

■ developed communication skills inside and outside the classroom

■ learned the new language which you will need if you are to describe

  – what you want to happen in classrooms
  – how you intend to evaluate the learning you observe

■ developed your skills of assessing pupil learning

■ challenged your own assumptions about how children learn

■ learned about a range of teaching strategies and the contexts of age and ability grouping for which they are appropriate

■ developed your skills of self-assessment and action planning.

GETTING STARTED

At this stage we need to think about:

- how best to plan lessons
- how to fit your planning strategies into the formats designed by your school and your Higher Education Institution (HEI).

Both the school and the HEI will use your planning notes as part of your assessment; it's important to get the format right.

Task 1: Establish the Ground Rules

- Transfer to your log all the information you have been given on how you are expected to set out plans.

- Sort out any conflict you observe in the process. Do people have different expectations of you? Question your HEI tutors, school mentors and teachers in whose classes you teach.

Figure 2.1 *Considerations for planning*

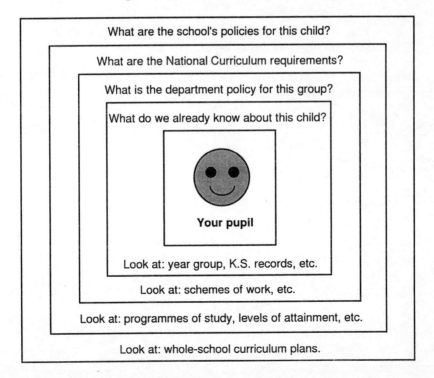

What are the school's policies for this child?

What are the National Curriculum requirements?

What is the department policy for this group?

What do we already know about this child?

Your pupil

Look at: year group, K.S. records, etc.

Look at: schemes of work, etc.

Look at: programmes of study, levels of attainment, etc.

Look at: whole-school curriculum plans.

Task 2: Explore the Issues

There is a lot to take into account, even in what seems to be the simplest of lessons. Experienced teachers hold many levels of planning in their heads at any one time. Learner teachers have to build up this repertoire.

- Observe one class with which you intend to work on *at least two occasions*. Discuss with the teacher the lessons you have seen and future lessons in which you may play a part.

- In your log, make notes of the different questions you will need to ask as you begin to take responsibility for planning.

- Figure 2.1 is designed to help you see how far your planning has to fit in with a wider pattern to complete the complex web of curriculum provision for pupils.

  You need to know how each layer contributes to the overall pattern of each individual pupil's learning. Use Figure 2.1 to structure a brief set of notes which bring together all you can find out about the individuals and class with which you are going to work.

- Look at the teacher's planning notes for this class. What do they tell you about the planning you need to do?

- Now look at your own skills. A SWOT analysis will help you; see Figure 2.2.

- Keep notes of:

  - the questions you identify
  - the information you gather
  - your SWOT analysis.

  Together they provide excellent evidence of your thinking and planning.

Figure 2.2 *A SWOT analysis for planning*

Strengths	What are my existing skills?
	Who can help me? How can I use colleagues in
	  – school?
	  – HEI?

Weaknesses	What problems do I have to overcome in terms of access to
	  – people?
	  – course requirements for pupils?
	  – internalising school policy?
	  – generating lesson ideas?

Opportunities	How wide is the range of lessons I might be able to teach? How do my existing skills meet the pupils' needs? What is my time-scale for working with them?
Threats	What are the problems/challenges involved in working with other teachers or students? What if we disagree about fundamental issues? Do I need to become a 'clone' of the teacher with whom I work? How do I find my own way of working with these pupils?

WHAT MAKES A GOOD PLAN?

Good plans start from certain 'givens' and map intended progress for individuals and the whole class. You need to *think about* all the issues identified in Figure 2.3 and to *research* your responses.

Figure 2.3 *Givens and intentions*

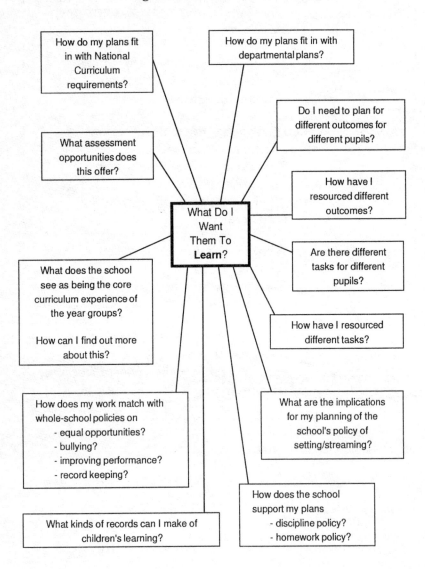

MAKING THE MOST OF YOUR OPPORTUNITIES

Teaching collaboratively allows you to:

- have time for close observation of pupils and their learning
- observe the effects of particular teaching styles and resources
- try new and, possibly, challenging strategies secure in the knowledge that you can, together, enable the class to work productively
- try on 'for size' other teachers' ways of working so that you can find your own ways of working and avoid simply 'cloning' others.

ACTION PLANNING IN COLLABORATIVE TEACHING

In Chapter 1 you considered the action planning process. You can use this strategy to structure your learning in collaborative teaching. Here's how you might use the process.

Stage one: what do you need to learn?

Think carefully and be honest – much has changed since you were at school. Remember that your memories are those of a pupil who had the potential to go on to Higher Education – you were not necessarily typical of the pupils you will teach.

So you should ask yourself what you need to learn about

- these pupils?
- their learning needs?
- the expectations the school has for them?

Stage two: how can you meet your needs?

A key issue here is how you plan to move from what you know and can do now to a future position in which you know more and can do more. This demands that you set yourself *targets* based on an analysis of what you know, your existing skills and your future opportunities.

Stage three: making it happen

Consider who might be able to help you:

- your lecturers and tutors in your HEI?
- the teachers and mentors in your school?
- fellow students?

How might they help you? By:

- giving you background details
- helping you plan specific activities
- noting and valuing your planning process
- troubleshooting – 'with this group I wouldn't ...'
- sharing objectives – 'together we might ...'
- helping you identify and adapt resources.

It is important that you are explicit as to what you need at this stage. Teachers are busy people and will often assume that all is fine unless you signal that you need help. The tutors from your HEI will only visit from time to time. You need to be ready to ask mentors for specific advice as and when you need it.

Stage four: being an action researcher

Collaborative teaching does not require you to take the full responsibility for managing a whole class. Instead it offers you the opportunity to:

- reflect

- plan

- act

- evaluate.

It is important, then, that you take this opportunity to explore the cycle from planning to delivery and *evaluation* and learn as much as possible from it. Task 3 will help you do this.

Evaluation involves five steps:

- setting learning goals:
  - for yourself
  - for your pupils
- Identifying what will be indicators of good learning. These are called *Performance Indicators* (PIs)
- devising ways to collect evidence as to how far you have achieved your PIs.
- Collecting and reviewing your evidence.
- Setting new learning goals.

and so on . . .

Task 3: A Way to Evaluate

- Consider the learning needs of five pupils in a class which you are expected to teach. Choose so that they offer a representative sample of the group.
- Think about the lesson and how you might evaluate it.
  - What might you expect each of your five pupils to learn?
  - How might you recognise this learning? What will they say, do and write to demonstrate their learning?

These questions form the basis of your PIs.

  - How will you collect and record your evidence? What evidence will you ask your collaborating teacher to collect and record?
  - How will you review this evidence with your collaborating teacher?
- Collect your evidence from the lesson. Use your log to review this material. What does it tell you about:
  - your own learning?
  - your pupils' learning?

■ Which goals have been achieved? What new goals seem appropriate?

MANAGING DIFFICULT SITUATIONS

CASE STUDY

Ann is working with a number of teachers in a school. Her timetable includes a number of lessons in which she is to work with Peter, the head of department. To her dismay, she finds that the classes she shares with him are the ones in which she has least opportunity to be creative.

She sees her problems as being that:

■ he doesn't share his planning with her. She begins to wonder how far he does plan!

■ over the years he has come to expect and accept a low level of performance from pupils in his subject area

■ he tells her that his methods are the only ones that will work with 'this kind of pupil' and that if she uses similar strategies she will be seen by colleagues in school and in the HEI as doing very well given the circumstances.

Here are some responses that Ann might consider.

1. Ignore what Peter has in mind and design much more challenging lessons. She would need to think about:

■ how the classes might respond to her new approach

■ how she might convince Peter that her plans are worth while

■ how she might prepare colleagues in school and in the HEI for the conflict they might observe

■ the types of conflict she might expect.

2. Stick with the approach offered by Peter and try to do it well. She would need to think about:

■ how she might plan her work without his involvement

■ how she might prepare her work for her own assessment, given these constraints.

3. Call in the cavalry! Enlist the aid of the people responsible for initial teacher training in the school and in the HEI, and use them to help her solve the problem. She would need to think about:

■ what she might wish to raise as concerns

■ how far her perspective will be seen as valid

■ how far all parties will need to work with Peter and will be reluctant to challenge him.

Task 4: What would you do?

■ Imagine you are Ann. Explain in your log:
   - your general strategy
   - whom you would need to consult
   - what outcomes you would want from these consultations
   - how you might organise your planning
   - how you would try to get the necessary level of support.

■ Discuss your strategy with at least one other learner teacher:
   - what emerges as controversial?
   - what strategies do you agree on?

This task highlights a *problem-solving strategy*, in which you have found ways forward by:

■ *identifying* key elements of the problem

■ *prioritising* those which need to be dealt with

■ *selecting* appropriate strategies

■ *briefing* selected allies to enable you to work through the situation.

PREPARING FOR ASSESSMENT

In order to become a qualified teacher you will need to participate in a number of assessment activities. You will need to gather information and evidence about your work to inform:

■ your own self-assessment

■ the assessments which must be made by your mentors.

These assessments must relate to the list of competences expected of newly-qualified teachers as described by the DFE (see Appendix 1). This chapter has focused on specific competence statements from the DFE, listed below. You may find your HEI has developed its own version of these competence statements; they will cross-reference with the DFE statements. You will need to match your work with the description of competence your HEI uses.

Subject application

Newly-qualified teachers should be able to

■ produce coherent lesson plans which take account of NCATs* and of the school's curriculum policies (SA 1)
■ employ a range of teaching strategies appropriate to the age, ability and attainment level of pupils (SA 4)
■ demonstrate ability to select and use appropriate resources, including information technology (SA 7).

Assessment and recording of pupils' progress

Newly-qualified teachers should be able to:

■ assess and record systematically the progress of individual pupils (A&R 3).

Further professional development

Newly qualified teachers should have acquired in initial training the necessary foundation to develop:

■ an ability to develop effective working relationships with professional colleagues and parents, and to develop their communication skills (FPD 3)

- an awareness of individual differences, including social, psychological, developmental and cultural dimensions (FPD 4)

- a self-critical approach to diagnosing and evaluating pupils' learning, including a recognition of the effects on that learning of teachers' expectations (FPD 7).

* NCATs – National Curriculum Attainment Targets

Each activity you undertake provides a rich and varied source of evidence. The kinds of evidence that are likely to be available are:

- your plans – and the notes you have made to justify your choices

- your observation notes – they can illustrate your perception of key issues

- your log – offers documentation of self-critical thinking

- your accounts of tasks undertaken in response to this book

- notes on the marking you have done

- teaching material you have used or devised, together with your evaluations of the process

- children's work – produced as a result of your teaching

- notes of feedback
  – which teachers or peers have offered to you
  – which you have offered to peers

- action plans resulting from this feedback and self-assessment

- SWOT analyses you have done

- any other reflections and evaluations you have undertaken.

You should ensure that you:

- collect evidence systematically

- get *validation* wherever possible. This means that if you do something well, a teacher or HEI tutor needs to record that she/he has observed you doing so

- consider what your evidence proves in terms of the competences against which you are to be assessed
- select key items which illustrate your competence
- identify areas in which you need to collect further evidence
- revisit this evidence base from time to time and replace your key items with ones which better represent your growing skills.

Task 5: Tracking Evidence

- Choose two or three collaborative teaching activities you have been part of recently.
- Bring together the evidence generated by these activities and ensure it is validated wherever possible.
- Find five pieces of evidence which best illustrate your competence in different areas.
- Enter this evidence on a grid like the one in Figure 2.4.
- Consider:
  - does the evidence you have collected give good coverage of the competences you need to demonstrate?
  - does the evidence you have collected represent the full range of the work you have been doing?

You will need to develop your own version of the grid we have designed for you.

Appendix 2 shows you how to develop this model across your whole course. Appendix 3 maps the ways in which the tasks in this book enable you to meet all the assessment requirements of the DFE competences.

Figure 2.4 *Evidence base*

	Activity 1	Activity 2	Activity 3
DFE Competence Statements	Shared planning of series of lessons to cover specific NCAT for Year 9	Planned and taught activities for a group of very able pupils for two weeks within mentor's lesson for Year 9	Taught an 'A'-level class without dictating notes!
Subject Knowledge	*Item 1:* Notes prepared in advance of planning meeting show SK 1 and SK 2*	*Item 1:* Additional reading booklet prepared to extend key concepts of lessons shows SK 1 and SK 3	
Subject Application	Notes as above show SA 2 and SA 4 *Item 2:* Plan for lesson 3 of series endorsed by supervising teacher shows SA 1 and SA 7	Booklet shows SA 5 and SA 6 *Item 2:* Extension activities in booklet show SA 3 and SA 4 *Item 3:* Feedback notes from mentor make reference to SA 3, SA 5 and SA 6	
Class Management	Notes and plan as above demonstrate CM 1	Feedback notes from mentor make reference to CM 2 and CM 4	
Assessment and Recording of Pupil Progress	*Item 3:* Contributed an assessment activity for lesson 4, shows A&R 3 and A&R 4	*Item 4:* Evaluation report written for mentor shows A&R 1 and A&R 2 *Item 5:* Marking of extension activities shows A&R 4 and A&R 5	
Further Professional Development	*Item 4:* Evaluation questions for lesson 3 show FPD 7 *Item 5:* Presence at dept meetings and contributions to overall planning minuted, shows FPD 1 and FPD 3	Booklet shows FPD 4 and FPD 5. Booklet available for all staff to use, shows FPD 3 Evaluation report shows FPD 7	

* See Appendix 1 for a full version of the DFE Competence Statements, numbering and code system.

LOOKING FORWARD

This chapter has focused on the areas highlighted in the following chart:

Core Skills	Teaching Competences

Action planning
 Problem solving
 Self-assessment
 record keeping
 observation
 using feedback
 using information
 Collecting evidence
 Working with adults
 Working with pupils
 analysis
 Evaluating
 Managing people
     time
       resources
	Subject Knowledge
	 —

	Subject Application *SA 1* *SA 4* *SA 7*
	Classroom Management CM 2 CM 4
	Assessment and Recording of Pupils' Progress A&R 3
	Further Professional Development FPD 3 FPD 4

The next chapter will help you begin to prepare for, deliver and evaluate lessons in which you are the key teacher – in which you 'fly solo'. Before you start, you need to think ahead.

Task 6: Think Ahead

Identify what you anticipate will be the differences between teaching collaboratively and teaching alone. Identify which skills you will need to develop to meet this new challenge.

Action plan your learning:

- What are your learning needs?

- How can you meet them?

- How can others help you?

- How might you evaluate your learning?

Flying Solo

INTRODUCTION

Bringing together all the skills of teaching so that you can teach a whole class for a whole lesson and, eventually, for a series of lessons can seem a daunting task. You will already have many of the skills you need and earlier chapters have addressed several aspects of the task of teaching.

The purpose of this chapter is to help you:

- bring together all the skills you have been developing

- understand, and include in your learning, new aspects of teaching involving managing the whole class and the classroom

- develop a broader view of teaching and your role as a teacher.

In this chapter, you are invited to undertake activities in which you will:

- extend the skills you developed earlier for planning and reflecting on your own learning

- explore the skills you need for classroom management

- learn ways to make the best use of the feedback that you will be offered by others – teachers in school, HEI tutors and, possibly, fellow students – who will witness your teaching and will want to help you learn from your experience

■ maintain a body of evidence which demonstrates your competence as a teacher and helps you plan new targets for yourself.

MAPPING YOUR LEARNING

As you work through this chapter and begin to teach by yourself, you need to value and record your learning. Take time to think about how far you have:

■ extended the skills you explored in collaborative teaching

■ learned to balance all of the different challenges involved in teaching whole classes

■ developed learning materials and strategies which meet the needs of all pupils

■ learned about yourself as a teacher

■ learned to make use of feedback from a range of sources.

GETTING STARTED

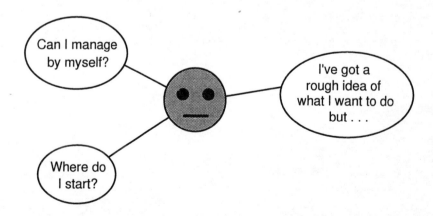

When you begin teaching by yourself, you also take on the responsibility for planning and preparing the lessons. Others can help you in setting the goals for the lesson, give you ideas about ways of teaching it and suggest resources to use in it, but only you can decide the detail of a plan which you feel happy to implement.

You will need to find a way of planning which suits the way you and your school like to work and which also fits the documentation you are expected to produce for your course and your assessment.

Planning a lesson is a complex task which can be tackled in a variety of ways. In Chapter 2 we suggested you gather together examples of lesson plans used by the teachers and tutors around you in school and in your HEI. In these plans there will be a variety of formats and different kinds of detail. Most plans will look something like the one in Figure 3.1.

Lesson plans should all have certain key features:

- a statement of aims or rationale for the lesson

- the objectives and outcomes anticipated, including reference to the National Curriculum

- descriptions of learning activities and resources

- pupil monitoring and assessment strategies – formal or informal

- a time plan

- a procedure for evaluating the lesson.

Task 1: Looking at Plans

- Examine the plans of some lessons you have observed or collaborated in teaching.

- Identify each of the features shown in Figure 3.1 in these plans.

- Some plans may not address all of these features. How would you redraft them to make their intentions explicit?

Figure 3.1 *Features of a lesson plan*

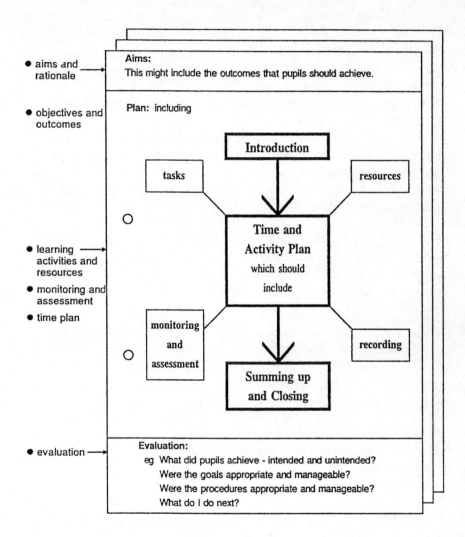

THE PROCESS OF PLANNING

Stage one: Look before you leap

It is a good idea to get a picture of the group you are teaching, their prior experience and likely expectations of the lesson, the place of the lesson in a wider scheme of work and any additional aspects of the curriculum.

Task 2 in Chapter 2 offered a way of mapping this territory for your lesson. You can use its approach whenever you begin thinking about a lesson plan, especially for the first time you teach a class, but remember to keep your 'map' up to date as the class progresses.

Stage two: Clarify the essentials

The essentials are the *actual learning needs* of the pupils (in the context of this lesson) and the *specific learning goals* which are appropriate for them. The *action planning* process described in Chapter 1 can be adopted here; the questions you need to consider are set out in Task 2.

These two steps will give you a set of aims and objectives for your lesson with a sound rationale for your choices.

Stage three: Decide on a strategy

At this stage, you need to convert aims and objectives into a choice of teaching approach for your lesson, indicating pupil activities and their outcomes. As a learner teacher, it is especially helpful to be clear about the outcomes you intend pupils to achieve and any other criteria by which the success of your lesson might be judged. These will help you plan, with the teacher or tutor observing you, how the lesson will be monitored, what feedback you would like to get and how you and your supervisor will review it afterwards.

Stage four: Prepare a plan

Now you are ready to fill in the detail of your lesson plan. You will need to be specific about how you are going to teach the lesson; the tasks you are going to set, the resources you are going to use, the time you are going to allow, how you are going to open the lesson and how you are going to close it.

Stage five: Decide how to review it

As a learner teacher, you will need to be clear about how you are going to judge the success of your lesson, whether or not you are being formally observed. You should use the criteria that were part of your strategy and you should also consider what *you* have learned from the experience. Also remember there will be many learning outcomes for you and your pupils which you were not expecting.

The next two tasks will help you plan a lesson using the steps just described. Keep the notes you make at each stage of planning, as well as your final plan: they can provide useful evidence for your assessment in a number of the competence areas, eg Subject Application (SA 1, SA 2, SA 3), Classroom Management (CM 1), Assessment and Recording (A&R 3, A&R 4), Further Professional Development (FPD 7). (See Appendix 1 for numbering and codes system.)

Task 2: Clarifying Essentials

■ Choose a lesson you are soon going to teach by yourself.

■ Collect together all the information you have about:

 – the class you are going to teach – you will probably have done a 'map' of the issues and needs as in Task 2 of Chapter Two
 – the overall programme containing the lesson you are expected to teach.

■ Use an *action planning* approach to identify the most appropriate aims and objectives for the lesson, by answering these questions:

 – What are the pupils' learning needs? Where are they now and what do I want them to work towards?

- What are appropriate aims for this lesson?
  What should I ask the pupils to learn/do next and what can I do to help them?
- How will I do this? What information should I give them, what kinds of activities can I give them?
- How will I know if they are successful? What outcomes do I expect and what evidence could I collect?

These questions will give you the aims, outcomes and criteria with which to start planning your lesson. They will also give you ideas about your teaching approach and the specific tasks you can set for the pupils.

Task 3: Preparing a Plan

■ For a lesson that you are about to teach, clarify the aims and objectives and the particular pupil tasks you are going to use. Stages one, two and three of the planning process will help you do this.

■ Now devise a provisional sequence and time plan for the lesson. Remember, you will have to allow time for each of the following:

- opening the lesson
- explaining the tasks and procedures you wish to be followed
- the tasks themselves
- any change-over periods
- closing the lesson.

■ Next consider the implications of these tasks and the time plan for:

resources   –   what will you need?
                                                –   how will you distribute them?

monitoring activities   –   how will you check progress with the tasks?

	–	where do you have the flexibility to adjust your timings?
	–	where and when will you need to be especially vigilant?
assessing learning	–	how will you check what pupils are learning from the tasks?
	–	with which tasks are pupils likely to experience the most difficulty?
recording	–	what records of the lesson will you keep? (Any changes to plans, any impressions?)
	–	what records of individual pupils' progress should you keep?
	–	how will you collect the information for these records?

■ Finally go back to your activity and time plan and make any adjustments you think are needed to make it more manageable.

You now have a lesson plan! Agree your plan with your mentor. At the same time agree how the lesson will be evaluated – by your observer, perhaps, as well as yourself – and set a time for the review. Now teach the lesson and review it. How effective was your plan?

MAKING THE MOST OF YOUR OPPORTUNITIES

One of the richest learning resources you will be offered at this stage is the feedback provided by the experienced teachers or tutors who observe your lessons.

FINDING A FRAME FOR FEEDBACK

Classrooms are busy places and any observer will have a great deal to take in and evaluate. Whether intentionally or unintentionally, their observations will be selective, so much can be gained by offering them a frame or focus for their observations. You can shape your own learning by negotiating a focus and criteria which match your current interests and concerns.

Task 4: Identifying Concerns

■ Look back in your log at recent entries about your classroom experience for ideas about your learning needs. Things you might look for are:

  – references to individual pupils and the concerns they reflect
  – types of activities – for strengths, weaknesses and variety
  – aspects of classroom management – difficult situations, less than successful strategies.

■ What are the issues that seem to recur? Note them in your log. Which seem the most significant?

■ Which should you prioritise for seeking feedback and advice from your observers?

Let us assume that classroom management is an area causing you some concerns. The DFE has described competence in classroom management in the following way:

Class management

Newly-qualified teachers should be able to:

■ decide when teaching the whole class, groups, pairs, or individuals is appropriate for particular learning purposes;

■ create and maintain a purposeful and orderly environment for the pupils;

■ devise and use appropriate rewards and sanctions to maintain an effective learning environment;

■ maintain pupils' interest and motivation.

These may seem somewhat unspecific and probably do not cover all the aspects you have identified for yourself; the competence statements provided on your own course may be more helpful.

However plainly competence statements are set out, your skill in them can only be judged by focusing on specific actions and events that take place in your classroom. What might these be? A good way for you to begin to answer this is for you to describe how your classroom might look and sound if you are truly competent in all of these areas. What signs, or *indicators*, of your competence might there be?

Good indicators are **SMART**

Specific
Measurable – or at least easy to record objectively
Achievable
Reliable
Time efficient – for the recorder!

Task 5: Selecting Indicators

■ Choose one of the competence statements for classroom management (from the DFE list or from the list provided by your HEI).

■ Describe five things that would characterise your classroom if it/you were as described in the competence statement. It may help you to think about a particular lesson you are about to teach.

■ Identify how one would recognise each of these characteristics at particular points in the course of the lesson:

– what would you be doing?
– what would the pupils be doing?
– what would their work be like?

■ What could you ask your observer to record and feed back to you after the lesson? Bear in mind anything you ask your observer to feed back will need to be SMART.

- As with the planning task, make sure you discuss and agree with your observer the indicators you wish to have recorded before you teach the lesson.
- Now teach the lesson and follow it with the feedback session.

MANAGING THE FEEDBACK SESSION

If you have followed Tasks 4 and 5, you will have taken the opportunity to shape your own learning by requesting your observer to provide particular kinds of evidence showing the extent of your effectiveness in areas about which you are unsure. The purpose of doing this is to help you clarify your further learning needs and set new targets. The feedback discussion should be based on these positive purposes.
  The ground rules for feedback sessions are:

- *Hear* what is being said – without jumping to conclusions or seeking to justify

- *Clarify* your understanding – by 'playing back' what you have heard to be sure it is what was intended

- *Acknowledge* your observers' point of view and that they are trying to be helpful

- *Ask* for further information/explanation of any aspect that you are not happy with – the interview is for your benefit and understanding

- *Think* about what has been said and what it means.

You can consider the implications of the feedback with your observer, or with a mentor at a different time, or on your own. A SWOT analysis as described in Chapter 2 can be helpful for this reflection (see Task 6).

Task 6: Using Feedback

- Having listened to your feedback, decide:
  - what are your **S**trengths and what are your **W**eaknesses?
  - what **O**pportunities do you have in the near future to focus again on this aspect of your competence?
  - what are the **T**hreats (difficulties you might encounter) which might limit your improvement in this aspect?

- Identify a suitable opportunity to look again at the focus you chose for feedback and design new indicators which will help you to identify those aspects you need to strengthen.

- Record these ideas in your log so that they can inform your future plans for making the most of your feedback.

MANAGING DIFFICULT SITUATIONS

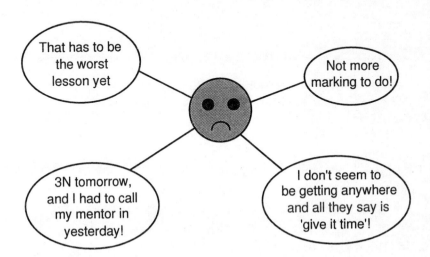

CASE STUDY 1

Paul is teaching a series of lessons with a Year 10 group which contains a small boisterous element. Two boys who have been on work experience return and join this group. They have become distinctly rowdy and obviously are no longer on task. His attempts to persuade them gently to settle down have proved unsuccessful. In exasperation he has threatened a detention if they do not return to the task and the reply has come, 'We're not coming to a detention from you, you're only a student.'

Task 7: Taking Timely Action

Consider Paul's situation:

- What options does he have?

- What does he need to know to make this decision? (What information about the department or the school would be relevant at this point?)

- What would be the *least* helpful thing to do at this stage?

- What would *you* do now? Who if anyone would you inform? When? How?

The story continues

Unfortunately the confrontation draws the attention of the rest of the class and Paul starts to lose his temper. He shouts that the whole class is in detention.

This does subdue the class but there is a general groan and muttering before they return to their work. Things continue quietly, but small incidents of disruption continue until just before the bell goes.

- What are Paul's options now?

- What advice would you offer him?

- Ask yourself the same questions as before and try to decide upon the most constructive thing to do to ensure that the next lesson can take place in a more productive atmosphere.

Enter the cavalry

Paul's mentor comes into the room to observe how the class is dismissed. Paul berates the class again in front of his mentor. He publicly asks the mentor to come to the class detention. His mentor agrees, if somewhat reluctantly, and the class is dismissed.

Paul probably did not need to get in this deep.

- Identify four or five points in the story at which Paul had available courses of action other than the ones he chose.

- What has he gained and what has he lost by enlisting the grudging support of his mentor for the detention?

- What would have been a more constructive approach to enlisting support from his mentor?

CASE STUDY 2

Paula has taught a number of lessons on her own and although she knows her mentor has been keeping an eye on the classes, he never seems to be around afterwards to discuss them with her. The most she gets from him are general reassurances that she's 'doing ok' and has 'nothing to worry about'. Her fellow student says she ought to be flattered since, on one occasion, her mentor even said she was better than most of the teachers in the department. However, Paula knows she could improve considerably if only she could get some specific feedback on different aspects of her teaching.

What would you do in Paula's situation? You will need to consider a number of aspects of the situation before you can answer.

First, Paula needs to be clear about the purpose of the feedback she is seeking. Then she needs to consider whether there are other sources of this feedback, where and for which purposes. Finally, she needs to consider how she can get more from her mentor.

Here are some ideas which might be useful should you find yourself in such a situation.

What are the functions of feedback?	evidencing success and achievements
	reflecting on teaching and learning
	target setting for new learning
Where else might I get feedback?	using a log and reviewing entries
	discussion with other students or teachers
	using other ways to 'record' lessons (tape, video, pupil feedback)
How can I get more from my mentor?	providing a specific frame for feedback, as in Task 4
	clarifying learning needs in an *action plan*
	using competence statements to justify request for specific help from mentor
	being assertive about the importance of continued learning for your future

PREPARING FOR ASSESSMENT

By now, you will have accumulated a considerable volume of documentation about your learning. In Chapter 1 we gave some tasks to introduce the idea of evidence; in Chapter 2 we offered you a way of mapping your evidence. This is your evidence base for the assessment process. You will need to select those items which best illustrate the quality of your planning, teaching and evaluation. One way to do this is to focus on a particular competence (as described by your course or from the DFE competences) and collect together evidence of your practice in this respect.

Good evidence:

■ gives a clear picture of this competence in specific areas

■ is a reliable indicator of this competence – can you really claim the credit for this outcome?

■ demonstrates that you have achieved the necessary standard.

Remember you could use pupils' work, the records of your pupils' assessments, materials you have produced, your log and your notes as well as formal lesson plans, observation and feedback documents from the teachers and lecturers who are assessing you.

Task 8: Presenting the Evidence

Imagine your HEI tutor is coming to meet your mentor so that they can begin to work with you to complete your final assessment. They have asked to meet you so that you can bring them up to date on your planning, teaching and evaluation. Your tutor is also hoping to be able to use the information from this discussion when she constructs her reference about you.

■ Select one area of competence (either from the DFE list or those for your course) which you would like to talk about in this session.

■ Plan how you will present yourself by:

 – collecting material from your evidence base which illustrates your competence in this area

- selecting that evidence which is clear, reliable, authentic and to a good standard
- considering the collection of evidence as a whole to decide:
  - does it present an overall picture of you which is fair?
  - is it strong enough to convince someone who has not seen much of your teaching?
  - does it cover all the aspects of the competence you are focusing on? (If not, what will you say or do to complete the picture?)

■ Confirm your selection of evidence by discussing it with one of your peers or another teacher who is not involved in the formal assessment.

CASE STUDY 3

Victoria is preparing for just such a meeting. She uses her log to record her selection of evidence to demonstrate her competence in the area of subject application. Figure 3.2 represents her summary of the evidence.

Figure 3.2 *Victoria's log*

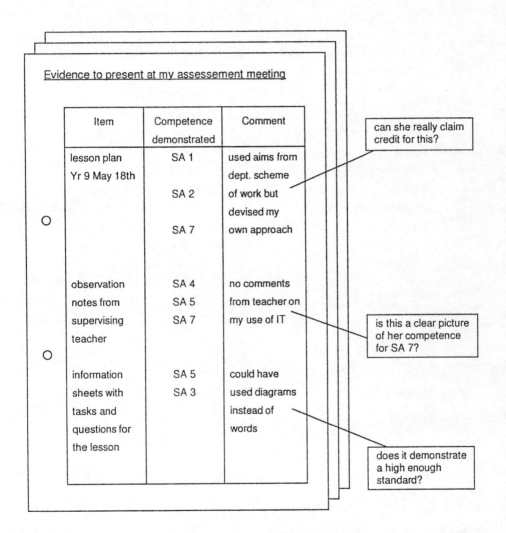

Evidence to present at my assessement meeting

Item	Competence demonstrated	Comment
lesson plan Yr 9 May 18th	SA 1	used aims from dept. scheme
	SA 2	of work but devised my
	SA 7	own approach
observation notes from supervising teacher	SA 4 SA 5 SA 7	no comments from teacher on my use of IT
information sheets with tasks and questions for the lesson	SA 5 SA 3	could have used diagrams instead of words

can she really claim credit for this?

is this a clear picture of her competence for SA 7?

does it demonstrate a high enough standard?

LOOKING FORWARD

This chapter has given focus to the areas highlighted in the following chart:

Core Skills	Teaching Competences

Action planning
Problem solving
Self-assessment
record keeping
Observation
Using feedback
Using information
Collecting evidence
Working with adults
Working with pupils
analysis
Evaluating
Managing people
       time
       resources
	Subject Knowledge
	SK 2

	Subject Application *SA 1* *SA 3* *SA 4* *SA 7*
	Classroom Management *CM 1* *CM 3*
	Assessment and Recording of Pupils' Progress *A&R 1* *A&R 3* *A&R 4*
	Further Professional Development *FPD 3* *FPD 4* *FPD 5* *FPD 7*

Task 9: Bridge the Gaps

Select two of the DFE competence areas.

■ Use a grid like the one shown in Appendix 2 and the activities described in Chapter 2 Task 2 and Chapter 3 Task 8 to map the evidence you are accumulating.

■ Identify competences for which you have little evidence.

- Think about where and when you might generate evidence for these competences later in your course.

- Make a note of these needs and potential opportunities in your log. You could use the *action planning* strategy introduced in Chapter 1 to begin planning for these opportunities.

The next chapter will help you bring together what you know about your own learning and that of your pupils so that:

- you can prepare to hand back the classes you have taught

- prepare for your final assessment.

Task 10: Think Ahead

- Which of the core skills will you most need to develop for this new challenge?

- *Action plan* how you will develop them.

CHAPTER 4

Bringing It Together

INTRODUCTION

The pupils' time with you is relatively short. It is your responsibility to hand over to the teachers who must continue to work with these pupils the following sets of information:

- details of lessons you have taught
- full records of pupil assessment within the programme you have taught.

You will need to allow time before the end of your teaching programme to collect evidence about:

- pupil achievement
- your own learning.

The purpose of this chapter is to help you:

- reflect on your own learning and how you are progressing towards your final assessment
- develop record keeping skills
- develop time management skills

In this chapter you are invited to undertake activities which will help you:

■ analyse your learning so far and

  - identify gaps in this learning
  - find strategies to fill these gaps
  - review your evidence base about your learning and find ways of demonstrating your competences.

■ support your pupils' learning by

  - planning to be on target to hand over lesson programmes which are complete and coherent. This will enable regular teachers to plan to complement your work.
  - developing your record keeping skills. You will need to hand over complete sets of records for all pupils. Are you ready to do this?

■ manage your time so that you meet all your deadlines.

MAPPING YOUR LEARNING

As you work through this chapter and begin to bring your work with your classes to a conclusion, you need to value and record your learning. Take time to think about how you have:

■ extended your teaching skills

■ met the targets you set yourself

■ developed the skills of assessing pupils' learning.

GETTING STARTED

Learner teachers are often so preoccupied with managing day-to-day in the classroom that they sideline the crucial area of assessment. You will need to demonstrate competence in this area. Here's how the DFE describes what is involved:

Assessment and recording of pupils' progress

Newly-qualified teachers should be able to:

■ identify the current level of attainment of individual pupils using NCATs, statements of attainment and end of key stage statements where applicable

■ judge how well each pupil performs against the standard expected of a pupil of that age

■ assess and record systematically the progress of individual pupils

■ use such assessment in their teaching

■ demonstrate that they understand the importance of reporting to pupils on their progress and of marking their work regularly against agreed criteria.

You will also need to extend your skills of self-assessment and to develop further the evidence base of your growing competence.

Task 1: Identifying Trouble Spots

■ Review your work in assessing and recording pupils' learning. Take into account:

 – the DFE competence statements
 – relevant school policies.

■ Identify:

 – where you lack experience
 – problems you have failed to address
 – worries you have about your progress.

■ *Action Plan* how you will tackle these trouble spots. Decide:

 – what you need to learn
 – what you can do to meet this need
 – how you are going to do it
 – how you will show that you have done it.

Things you can do:

- *establish the 'bottom line'* – what is the school and departmental policy?
- *observe closely teachers' practice* – what do successful teachers do?
- *share marking* with another student-teacher so you can pool ideas
- *share your problems* with fellow students and lecturer/tutors at your HEI
- *plan your lessons so that you create assessment opportunities* – plan how to *use* your assessment to inform future planning
- *use opportunities within the school,* such as INSET days, assessment and moderation activities.

Before you leave your training school you will be expected to provide full details of:

- your teaching programme
- your pupils' learning.

Teachers, parents and pupils will all need you to be able to offer them appropriate information about your work and your pupils' progress. This will need to encompass a variety of pupil assessments.

It is not sufficient to rely on an end-of-topic test. You should be consciously and systematically collecting evidence of the learning of *individual* pupils through formal and informal means.

Figure 4.1 offers some pointers.

Figure 4.1 *Assessing individual pupils*

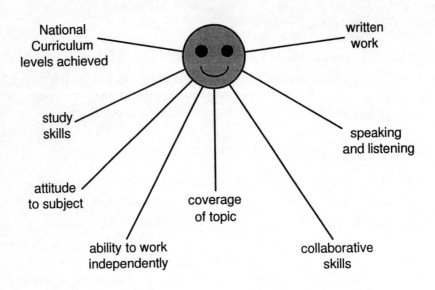

Task 2: Preparing an Account of Their Learning

- Think about each group for which you are responsible:
  - what types of evidence do you already have about pupils' learning?
  - what aspects of learning does this evidence cover?
  - do you have evidence about each pupil individually?
- Think about the time you have left.
  - what opportunities are available to complete this process?
- Identify the people you need to report to you:
  - who are they?
  - what do they need to know?
  - in what form?
- *Action Plan* a way of meeting these targets.

MAKING THE MOST OF YOUR OPPORTUNITIES

Deadlines are looming now. You will be aware that you need to tie up many loose ends. Be aware that:

■ you are accountable to the pupils you teach. They deserve a smooth transition to their work with their 'proper' teachers.

■ you have a limited time scale in which to observe and demonstrate your competences in terms of the DFE document (Appendix 1).

In order to meet your deadlines you will need to develop time management skills.

MAKING THE MOST OF YOUR TIME

Good *time managers* can:

- take time out
- prioritise
- distinguish between what is important and what is urgent
- set appropriate, realisable targets
- know when to stop
- know what is 'good enough'
- say no
- make short- and long-term plans
- alter them as things progress
- make lists.

CASE STUDY 1

Susan has been teaching solo a first-year group for six weeks and has three weeks to go. There are 30 children in this class, which includes a wide range of ability and achievement. She has to plan how to conclude the programme of lessons satisfactorily and how to record and report the learning that has gone on. There is a parents' evening in three weeks time and reports must be written within the next two weeks. Susan has to:

1 identify her assessment criteria
2 match them with National Curriculum criteria
3 plan her assessment strategy
4 find ways of recording her assessment
5 assess 30 students
6 write individual reports on each student.

What she needs is *Critical Path Analysis.*

Stage 1: Review the situation

Make a list of what needs doing.

– Are they all essential?
– Are all the tasks described?

Stage 2: Sequence

Put tasks in order.

– What needs doing first?
– Which tasks overlap?
– What cannot be done until last?

Stage 3: Cost time

– How long will each task take to do?
– What is the existing time scale?

Stage 4: Intermediate deadlines

Now plan backwards.

– Start from your deadline and the task which must be done last.
– Work backward to the present time.
– Identify intermediate deadlines.

═══════════════════════ **Here is Susan's plan** ═══════════════════════

Week 3   –   complete assessment
         –   draft reports on all students
         –   check with mentor that reports are appropriate

Week 2   –   ensure appropriate evidence is available where
             necessary
         –   arrange for moderation within department

Week 1   –   confirm assessment strategy and match with
             National Curriculum criteria
         –   plan assessment and recording opportunities.

MAKING THE MOST OF YOUR PUPILS' TIME

By now, you should have had the chance to 'fly solo', to take full responsibility for a class. Much of your energy will have been focused on this big challenge. However, you need to think beyond it and towards the all-elusive grand scheme.

If you were wise, you started with such a scheme, but it is only now that it is beginning to seem achievable. You will recognise the opportunities for incorporating wider aspects of your learning and students' learning within your scheme.

In Chapter 2, you considered how your planning might take account of whole-school, cross-curricular issues, so that key areas are not neglected over a period of time.

You need to review:

■ how far your lessons have provided pupils with progression and continuity in developing skills such as literacy, numeracy and information technology as well as subject-specific skills, knowledge and concepts.

■ how far your lessons have reflected whole-school policies on what should be the pupils' experience of school.

A review of this kind will help you provide evidence of how far you have met the following DFE competences:

Subject application

Newly-qualified teachers should be able to:

- ensure continuity and progression within and between classes and in subjects
- contribute to the development of pupils' language and communication skills.

Class management

Newly-qualified teachers should be able to:

- create and maintain a purposeful and orderly environment for the pupils
- maintain pupils' interest and motivation.

Further professional development

Newly-qualified teachers should have acquired in initial training the necessary foundation to develop:

- an awareness of individual differences including social, psychological, developmental and cultural dimensions.

Task 3: Planning to Meet Long-term Goals

- Examine the programme of lessons you have taught to a particular class:
  - go back to your original overall plan and any other guidance you were given on the aims of this programme. What were your long-term goals?
  - review how far the lessons you have taught have promoted these goals.
- In your log write about:
  - what you now think about the original long-term goals. Were they appropriate?
  - how might you rephrase them in the light of your experience to indicate realistic goals for this particular programme?
  - how each lesson contributed to the goals.

■ Assess how well the programme has provided pupils with:

  – continuity in their learning
  – progression in their achievements.

■ Use a *critical path analysis* to revise your plans for the rest of the programme in the light of this review.

MANAGING DIFFICULT SITUATIONS

CASE STUDY 2

Sarla has had a very successful teaching experience so far. Her mentor initially observed lessons regularly and gave supportive feedback. Recently, however, the visits have become irregular and her mentor has been heard to say, 'I don't need to observe Sarla any longer. She is as good a teacher as anyone in the department'. Sarla feels she has still a lot to learn and in any case is worried as to how her mentor will be able to complete her assessment if he has inadequate evidence of her growing competence.

Sarla has at least three choices:

■ **Passivity** – She could wait for her mentor to guess what the problem is and respond.

■ **Aggression** – She could demand some attention and threaten to complain to all and sundry if she doesn't get it.

■ **Assertion** – She could ask for what she knows she needs – in a confident direct manner, but showing that she is clearly willing to negotiate an appropriate outcome.

In such a situation it would be helpful to be clear about:

- what needs changing
- what to ask for in order to change things
- how to broach the subject
- when and where to have the conversation with the mentor
- how to ensure that needs are met.

Task 4: Try It Out

If possible find a partner for this task.

■ Rehearse the conversation that might develop from each of these three starting points:

- Passive: I'm sorry to bother you, but would you mind ... ?

- Aggressive: Why have you ignored me? It's not fair ...

- Assertive: I would like more regular feedback. Will you visit at least one class next week ... ?

■ Identify ways in which confrontation might be avoided.

Assertiveness strategies can be used whenever you need to resolve conflict.

1. *Separate the problem from the person –*
   'I need an outsider's view of what is
   happening in my classroom'
   not
   'I need you to tell me'.

2. *Make sure there is something in it for both parties –*
   'I realise your time is short, however we both need
   the information on which my assessment will be based.'

3. *Don't be so focused on what you want to say that you can't hear the answer –*

> It might be necessary for the mentor to let off steam. You should see this for what it is and not overreact.

CASE STUDY 3

Bill has a problem. He has a child who has been ill. This has meant that he has not been doing as much work in the evenings as he needs to in order to keep on top of his marking and preparation. He has had many sleepless nights and has been finding it difficult to keep his mind on his work. Although his mentor and colleagues have been very sympathetic about his domestic situation, he has not been able to bring himself to admit just how far behind he has got. However, a parents' evening looms. He will be expected to show the parents their children's books. Already one child has asked why her work is never marked.

Bill needs to decide:

■ to whom he should speak, and when

■ what he should offer to do

■ what he should ask others to do if they are to help him

■ how he can ensure that he is ready for the parents' evening. He will need to be:

realistic	– a *critical path analysis* like the one you used in Task 3 might help him
assertive	– the guidelines which follow Task 4 might help him.

PREPARING FOR YOUR ASSESSMENT

It is important to be ready for your final assessment. Your preparation should include building a portfolio which offers evidence about your learning over the period of the course. Chapter 3 emphasised the need for you to judge the quality of this evidence. Is it *clear*, *reliable* and does it demonstrate your achievement of the *necessary standard*?

Task 5: Handing Over Classes

■ Build a portfolio which represents your work with at least one class

- make a list of what it should contain
- bring together all your portfolio material.

■ Use it to compile a report on the class which will form the basis of your handover meeting with their teacher.

A *class portfolio* might include:

■ register of attendance

■ homework records

■ weekly assessments against clear criteria

■ samples of pupils' work from a range of differing achievement levels

■ criteria for marking and grading this work

■ lesson plans in the context of the National Curriculum

■ overall plans for each group and plans for individuals within the group

■ evaluations of lessons

■ samples of written reports on pupils.

Portfolios of this kind will also provide excellent evidence to support your own assessment.

Task 6: Prepare for Review

Using a portfolio like the one compiled in Task 5:

- identify what evidence it offers of your competence in each of the areas specified in Appendix 1
- map this evidence on a grid like the one shown in Appendix 2
- use the evidence in your portfolio as the basis for a review meeting with your mentor in which you focus on the area of assessment and recording of pupils' progress.

LOOKING FORWARD

This chapter has given focus to the areas highlighted in the following chart.

Core Skills	Teaching Competences

Action planning
 Problem solving
 Self-assessment
 Record keeping
 observation
 using feedback
 using information
 Collecting evidence
 Working with adults
 Working with pupils
 Analysis
 Evaluating
 Managing people
     time
       resources
 Giving feedback to pupils
 Taking and sharing
 responsibilities
	Subject Knowledge
	 —
	
	 Subject Application
	 SA 1, SA 2, SA 6
	
	 Classroom Management
	 CM 2
	 CM 4
	
	 Assessment & Recording of Pupils' Progress
	 A&R 1 A&R 2 A&R 3
	 A&R 4 A&R 5 A&R 6
	 A&R 7
	
	 Further Professional Development
	 FPD 3
	 FPD 4
	 FPD 7

The next chapter will take you through the process of deciding to apply for a job, successfully making the application and preparing to start your first post.

Task 7: Think Ahead

- Which of the core skills will you most need to develop for this new challenge?
- *Action plan* how you will develop them.

CHAPTER 5

Moving On

INTRODUCTION

You may think you have only just got started on your training when people begin to ask you about applying for jobs. It is as well to start to think about this early on in the year without rushing into making applications. The decisions you make at this stage will affect your life for at least the next year and possibly for several years to come.

The purpose of this chapter is to help you:

- consolidate the learning you have undertaken
- present it positively to would-be employers
- plan ahead for further professional development.

This chapter invites you to engage in activities and gives you information which will help you to:

- decide when and where to apply for your first job
- make the most of your application
- decide whether you really want this job
- present yourself at your best in the interview
- think about how to handle potentially difficult situations in the process

- prepare for your new post
- plan your future professional development.

MAPPING YOUR LEARNING

Your learning in this chapter will not, in itself, provide evidence for you to demonstrate teaching competences, as described by the DFE or by your HEI. However, you will be offered the opportunity to bring together the wide range of learning in which you have been engaged during your course. A job interview is, after all, a kind of summative assessment. You will need to present your thinking and experience in a number of educational contexts, including all aspects of your teaching competence.

You will also have the opportunity in the course of this chapter to demonstrate that you have the ability to engage in the professional self-assessment which the DFE competences describe as the necessary foundation for further professional development:

Further professional development

Newly-qualified teachers should have acquired in initial training the necessary foundation to develop:

- an understanding of the school as an institution and its place within the community
- a working knowledge of their pastoral, contractual, legal and administrative responsibilities as teachers
- an ability to develop effective working relationships with professional colleagues and parents, and to develop their communication skills
- an awareness of individual differences, including social, psychological, developmental and cultural dimensions
- the ability to recognise diversity of talent including that of gifted pupils

- the ability to identify special educational needs or learning difficulties

- a self-critical approach to diagnosing and evaluating pupils' learning, including a recognition of the effects on that learning of teachers' expectations

- a readiness to promote the moral and spiritual well-being of pupils.

GETTING STARTED

There are certain peak times in the academic year for job opportunities. They are particularly abundant just before the Easter holiday and from early June onwards. You may be keen to get a job so that you can start to plan for your new career and possibly your new home. However, it is important not to rush into hasty and ill-considered commitments, but to research your options and preferences carefully.

LOOK BEFORE YOU LEAP

Stage one: Look at yourself

Note in your log:

- what have you liked most about being a member of a school?
- what have you liked least?
- what do these answers tell you about the kind of community you feel most comfortable in?

Stage two: Look at your circumstances

Are there aspects of your personal circumstances that might restrict your choices? There are many things to take into account, as the spidergram (Figure 5.1) illustrates. Use it to help you to:

- identify the factors which are important to you (these may include ones different from our example)
- put them in order of priority
- identify any factors which are non-negotiable.

Some people impose unnecessary restrictions on themselves; on the other hand, they may fail to take a realistic view as to how they can balance personal and work commitments. It is usually valuable to enlist the advice of someone who can help you be sure about these factors.

Stage three: Look at schools

Your choice of school may have a significant impact on your future. In planning a career it is important to be aware of what you will need to have done in order to get the *next* job. Already your experience has begun to shape your future opportunities. It may have been limited to some extent by the type of school(s) in which you have worked. You will have to make a conscious decision about the ways in which you wish to extend your experience.

- Use a grid like the one in Figure 5.2 to map:

    - the ways in which your current experience is limited
    - those areas in which you wish to extend your experience.

There may be things you can do now which will help to broaden your experience. Find out about:

- possibilities of visiting or teaching in other types of school, perhaps after your course is complete
- courses or projects you can undertake at your HEI
- students on your course whose experience differs from yours. (Can you exchange ideas?)

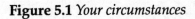

Figure 5.1 *Your circumstances*

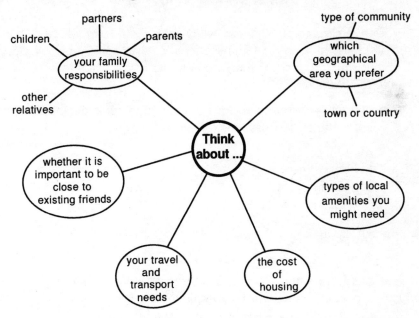

Figure 5.2 *Mapping your experience*

Aspects of school-based experience	Describe the experience you have had so far	How far do you think your experience to date might restrict your opportunities?	In which aspects do you wish to extend your experience?
single/mixed sex			
comprehensive/ selective			
fee-paying/ state-funded			
age range			
type of community			
size			

Task 1: Decide on Your Criteria

One strategy you can use when you need to make decisions which have long-term implications is to imagine yourself and your new situation at some point in the future when things have developed well.

■ Imagine yourself one year from now and complete the following sentences:

My school is . . .
My department is . . .
My classroom is . . .
My lessons are . . .
My colleagues are . . .
My pupils are . . .
My tutor group is . . .

■ Build, from this analysis, a set of criteria you would wish to use when considering a specific job.

■ Put the criteria in order of priority.

■ Think about when and how you might get the information you need about a job to make a judgement based on these criteria.

GETTING INFORMATION

From advertisements. Look at the appointments sections of publications like the *TES* (on Fridays) or Education *Guardian* (on Tuesdays). These are organised by phase, subject and responsibilities. Job advertisements contain a lot of information which will be of use to you as you begin the process of selection; see Figure 5.3.

From individual schools. Schools will send you, on request, both an application form and further details of the post and the school. These can be extremely revealing and it is important to read between the lines; see Figure 5.4.

Figure 5.3 *Reading advertisements*

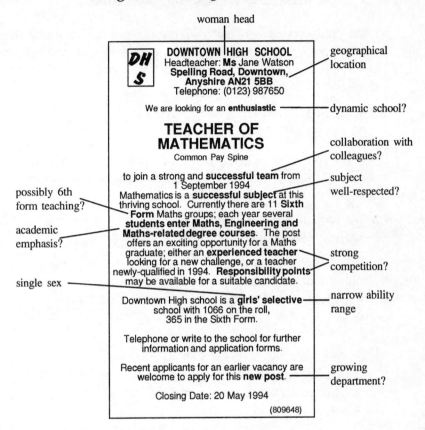

Figure 5.4 *Reading between the lines*

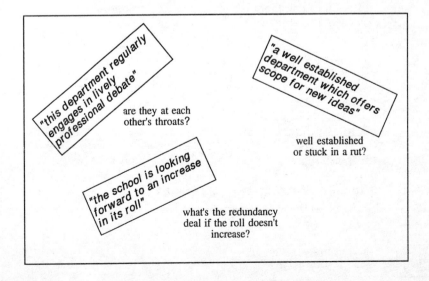

Task 2: Select Appropriate Schools

■ Analyse advertisements for your subject

- which jobs might fit your criteria from Task 1?
- if over a few weeks, you find that no jobs fit your criteria, go back to the drawing board.

■ Write to selected schools to ask for further details of the post and application forms.

■ Read through the information you receive from each school and underline in different colours statements which fit into each of these three categories:

- fits well with my criteria
- conflicts with my criteria
- not clear, need to find out more.

■ Think about the overall impression you have gained. How carefully do you think the people in the school have thought about this post and the kind of person they want to fill it?

■ Decide whether to continue with your application. If you are having difficulty deciding, discuss the information and your notes with a mentor or experienced teacher.

■ Even a thorough job description will leave you with many unanswered questions. Make a note of them. You will get a chance to ask them if you are invited to interview.

MAKING THE MOST OF YOUR OPPORTUNITIES

Schools will expect you to:

■ fill in a standard application form

■ support your application with a letter which should

- be no more than two sides of A4
- preferably be word-processed

    – give them some insight as to the kind of teacher
      you intend to be
    – tell them what you have to offer to this job and
      why you want it
    – tell them about your existing skills and experience.

They will also ask you to provide the names of two referees whose advice they may use in

■ shortlisting
■ appointing.

GETTING READY

There are at least six things you need to do in order to be ready to apply for jobs.

> **Stage one: Getting referees**

■ Who will be your referees? Your HEI must be one of them. Will your training school be the other? Are they the one to give you a reference? *Ask*

■ If your school is not prepared to give you a reference, who else might be prepared to support your application?

    – Previous university tutors?
    – People who have observed you working in related
      contexts?

■ Make sure you check out with people you think might help you in this respect that they are prepared to write a reference that will *support* your application. *Ask*

Make sure you let your referees know about the outcome of your interviews. They have invested time in you and have offered their professional judgement as to your potential.

> **Stage two: Use your references**

- What does your reference tell would-be employers about you? Most HEIs now make available their references to students. Schools and other referees may differ in their practice. *Find out what the policy is.*

- If you are allowed access to your reference, read it carefully and note what has been said about you. Think about how you might add to it in your interview. *Plan how to use it.*

> **Stage three: Use your profile**

Some candidates include their profiles in their application, others bring it to interview so they can provide evidence of their competences. Is yours ready to be used in this way? At the very least, you should use it to help you plan how you might present yourself at interview.

- Look at it with different eyes. What evidence does it contain about you? What would you wish to stress? What learning needs do you still have? *Know your strengths and weaknesses.*

> **Stage four: Sort out your CV**

- Schools will expect you to tell them about:

    - the schools you attended
    - your GCSE grades
    - your 'A' level grades
    - your degree; content and classification
    - your teacher training. Which HEI? What kind of course? In what kinds of schools?

- They will also ask about:

    - your previous employment history
    - your interests
    - any related experience such as voluntary work.

- You will find that there is only a short time between enquiring about a job and having to send in your application. You will need to have all the requisite 'standard' material readily available.

- Use the facilities at your HEI or, by agreement, in your school, to bring all this information together. *Put it on disk.*

Stage five: Fill in the application form

- You will find that it is often easier to do this by hand. Governors are often interested in seeing your handwriting! You can use your word-processed CV to give you easy access to all the information you require.

- Sometimes you might simply be asked to offer a CV, in which case you should offer all the information in stage four.

- Photocopy the application form and prepare a draft first. Check for accuracy and presentation.

- Only send the information that they requested. Usually this will consist of an application form and a supporting letter.

- Use continuation sheets if it is impossible to include all the information requested on the official form. Be selective and concise. Beware: some forms actually prohibit the use of continuation sheets.

Stage six: Prepare the letter of application

- Most would-be teachers have:
  - a high degree of credibility in their subject knowledge
  - experience of at least two schools
  - a degree of commitment to teaching.

- What makes you different?
  - your reference
  - your letter of application.

You need to understand that it is often your letter of application which gets you on the shortlist. Schools often only ask for references from those candidates they have shortlisted. So *your letter makes the difference.*

MAKING THE MOST OF YOUR APPLICATION

Your letter of application will need to address the following issues:

- why you have chosen to apply to this school
- what you can bring to the school
- how you envisage your wider role.

Why this school?

They *do not want to hear* that it is because it is near a railway station that will give you access to your family or sporting/recreational facilities. You need a better rationale for your choice. See the earlier sections of this chapter to help you identify this. You need to show that you have considered:

- the type of school
- its age range
- the community it serves.

Schools, heads and governors, quite rightly, think that their schools are special and they, ideally, would wish to appoint people who are particularly attracted to *their* school.

What can you bring?

They will have strong views on the kind of teacher they want to employ. They will want to know:

- what *principles* guide your thinking and practice in education

- what *you can deliver* – do you have areas of expertise which might be useful to them? Here you have several strengths:
  - your recent degree work makes you a potentially exciting 'A' level teacher
  - your course should have made you very aware of the demands and constraints of the National Curriculum
  - you may still be close in age to the pupils you are to teach, and this can be a big advantage

- you still see yourself as needing to learn. You are open to new ideas and should not be resistant to change. Think about your future learning needs and be prepared to talk about them
- the evidence you can offer them about your class room practice. It is easy to talk about your educational philosophy, but much harder to make it take flesh in classrooms. Build a portfolio of pupils' work, lesson plans, lesson evaluations and lesson observations, and take them with you to interviews.

Your wider role

Most schools to which you apply will want you to have an interest in and understanding of tutoring. They will value any previous experience of this role.

Policy and practice in this area differs from school to school. You will need to be aware of a range of models. You may find it helpful to supplement your lectures, seminars and school-based experience with wider reading. You will also find it helpful to think about the pastoral curriculum. Schools use a range of devices to plan and deliver:

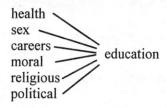

health
sex
careers
moral
religious
political
education

Sometimes there is a Personal and Social Education course; sometimes all these areas are integrated into the subject-specific curriculum. Think about the contribution your *subject* can make to the pastoral curriculum.

Pupils value their involvement in extracurricular activities. You may have a great deal to offer in this respect. Have you organised clubs, run pupil workshops, helped with drama productions, participated in team games? Think about whether and how you might present your experience or interest in such work.

Be careful. If you have found your teacher education course tiring, imagine how it will be when you have a full timetable and it's 'for real'. You will need to pace yourself. Don't offer to do things which you might find unduly demanding. Your new school will value your ability to balance work and play. You may have commitments to children or to other family members. You must be realistic as to what you can do.

Task 3: Go For It!

- Plan the crucial letter of application. Think about these points:
    - why this school?
    - why me?
    - what can I do?
    - how do I see my future professional needs?
- Write the letter

    - proof-read it; check spelling and grammar
    - keep it on disk so you can adjust it for different schools
    - ask other people to read it – other students', teachers at school and HEI tutors
    - think about how you might alter your letter in the light of their advice.

MAKING A GOOD DECISION

You need to know a certain amount about the school to which you are applying. You will need to:

- deal with specific questions during the interview
- be able to decide whether you would be happy to teach there.

Remember that you should be prepared to commit yourself for at least one year and ideally for two years. Remember, too, that the choices you make now will affect later career options.

You have already matched your existing experience and interests against the material sent to you by the school(s) to which you are applying. You will need further evidence and information before you make the crucial decision as to whether you would take this job if it were to be offered to you. You will need to spend time in the school, talking to teachers and pupils before you make this final decision.

Be prepared to state in the interview whether you will take this job. Very few governing bodies are willing to let you go away and think about it. They will want to appoint someone who is keen to work with them. They need to make the appointment on the day.

So, how do you check it out? Two options are available to you:

- you can visit the school before the interview date. You simply telephone and ask if you can do this. This option is most appropriate if:

  - you have already been shortlisted and invited to interview
  - the school is near enough for you to visit. You will not be able to claim travel expenses for a preliminary visit.

- you can look round the school and meet staff and pupils on the day of the interview.

Be aware that you will be assessed on everything you do and say. Schools will take note of:

- your letter asking for further details

- how you go about negotiating a pre-interview visit

- the questions you ask and the responses you make as you find out about the school.

Figure 5.5 gives advice on what *not* to do.

Figure 5.5 *Making a Good Impression*

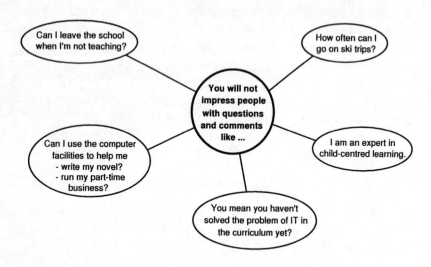

Task 4: Check It Out

- Decide whether you need to visit the school before the interview.

- Think again about your ideal school:

  - how would you recognise if this school fits your ideal?
  - what might it feel like for staff? For pupils?
  - what do you see as your future learning needs? What would you want your ideal school to offer you?
  - how far are you prepared to compromise? Which factors are negotiable? Which factors are non-negotiable?

- We can't all achieve our ideal. Think again about your criteria. Are you closing doors unnecessarily?

- Write down a list of questions that you want to ask during the information-gathering process. Refer back to the material earlier on in this chapter to help you in this process.

BE PREPARED FOR THE INTERVIEW

Who will be there?

You might expect to find some of the following people:

- the headteacher
- a deputy head
- the head of department or similar
- the LEA adviser
- lay governor(s)
- teacher governor(s).

What will they ask me?

They will have planned their questions in advance and will ask a series of

- common questions to all candidates
- specific questions based on your letter of application.

They should also offer you the opportunity to ask them questions.

Figure 5.6 *Interviewer's Expectations*

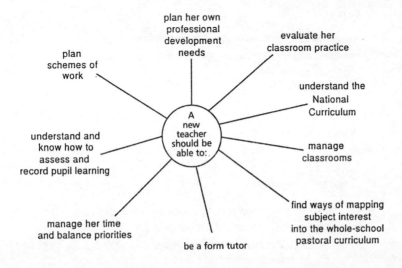

Task 5: Preparing For the Interview

■ Anticipate what they will ask you. Look at Figure 5.6. How can you convince the interviewing panel that you can do what they might expect of a new teacher?

■ Think about specific issues which might arise from your letter of application. Are you ready to deal with questions about them?

■ Prepare a set of index cards to help you through the interview. You can take them into the interview room. You might not use them but it can help to know they are to hand.

  – Write down on separate cards all the questions you think might be asked.
  – Check your questions with mentors and with fellow students who might already have been interviewed. Add any new questions.
  – Make brief notes on each card as to your response to each question.

■ Remember that the interview panel will need to know what you *can do as* well as what you think should be done. Prepare a portfolio of evidence to support your statements as to what you can do.

■ Be prepared for the challenging question. Governors often ask you to tell them about:

  – one lesson or module which went well
  – one lesson or module which caused problems
  – your strengths
  – your weaknesses.

Think carefully about how you might respond to these. You don't want to sound over-confident; on the other hand, governors will need to sense that you can deliver the goods. Take advice from mentors as to how you might balance these considerations.

■ Rehearse the interview if you can. Your mentor or HEI might give you the opportunity to have a trial interview. Ask for this and take detailed notes of the feedback you get.

MAKING THE MOST OF THE INTERVIEW

Most people find interviews very stressful. Remember that the purpose of the exercise is to allow you to show your strengths and to enable the interview panel to match what you have to offer against what they see as being the needs of the school. It is a *two-way process*.

Think of it as an opportunity for you to assess them as much as for them to assess you. Be honest about your strengths and weaknesses. The governors need to make a judgement as to whether and how far you can help the school develop. You need to decide how far you want to be part of the process.

MAKING THE MOST OF YOURSELF

Wear smart, conventional clothes. Schools need to know that you can 'play the game' and that you can present yourself in a way that pupils and parents find acceptable.

Listen to what the school tells you. There may be things which you would like to contest. Think carefully before you challenge people.

Tune in to what the school wishes to achieve. Does it match with your vision? If their vision is totally alien to you, then you would be justified in withdrawing from the interview. If you don't wish to withdraw, listen closely to what they are saying and match your potential responses to what seem to be the school's needs and interests.

Be flexible. You still have much to learn. Can this school help you in the process? What do you observe about its policy for teaching and learning? Can you imagine that you could work within the institution?

The shape of the interview day is likely to be as follows.

- You will be invited to the school along with a number of other candidates. Some might be 'internal' candidates, ie existing staff on temporary contracts or students who have done their training in the school.

- All candidates will normally be given a tour of the school and will be offered the opportunity to talk to staff and pupils.

- Remember that you will be assessed all the time you are in the school.

- The interview process will then begin. Each candidate will normally be interviewed for about half an hour. Normally, all the candidates stay in the school until a decision has been made.

- When everyone has been interviewed, the governors will begin to make their decision. This could take at least another half hour.

- The successful candidate will be called in to be offered the job.

- The governing body or the head teacher should offer unsuccessful candidates a debriefing on their interview. You should take this opportunity either on the day or later. You will need to know why you failed to get the job so that you can prepare for the next interview.

MANAGING DIFFICULT SITUATIONS

CASE STUDY 1

Tina, a biology teacher, is very keen to work in Downtown Comprehensive. She has done her training there and likes the school. Her daughter is happy in a local playgroup. There is a job available and the head of department has said she would welcome her application. All seems well. The problem is that the school is offering this post on the basis of a temporary contract for one year.

This is not an untypical problem. Schools for a variety of reasons need the flexibility which temporary contracts provide.

Think about Tina's options:

- what further information would she need to find out to help her make her decision?

■ how would you balance her need for this job in this school against the possibility of having to start to look elsewhere for another post?

–––––––––––––––––––––––– CASE STUDY 2 ––––––––––––––––––––––––

Bill has applied for a job at Downtown Comprehensive. He has got to the interview and is asked by a governor if he is prepared to put on the annual drama production. His child, James, is at playschool and his partner Susan is planning to train to be a teacher next year. They know that their time for James will be limited by Bill's job and Susan's commitment to her training. Bill very much wants the job. He likes the school, but he is worried about whether he can take on the extra curricular responsibilities.

Task 6: How Much Do I Have to Offer to Do?

■ Anticipate this kind of question. What would your response be? Where might you get further advice:

  – your training school?
  – your HEI?
  – other sources?

■ Imagine yourself in your new job:

  – how will you organise your time?
  – what priorities will you have?
  – complete a grid like the one in Figure 5.7 to help you begin the process of identifying what you can and cannot take on.

Figure 5.7 *What will my week be like?*

Must do	Should do	Want to do
marking	exercise	read
preparation	continue reading about education	entertain
attend meetings	have time with family/friends	relax
go to parents' evenings	keep up with my subject	go to cinema and theatre
have further training	sleep eight hours per night!	develop a hobby/interest

CASE STUDY 3

Catherine has applied for a job and has been interviewed but was not successful. She prepared carefully for the interview and does not know why she failed to get the job. The headteacher has offered to debrief her. She has to decide what she needs to find out at the debriefing.

Task 7: Getting Debriefed

■ Plan the list of questions you would want to ask a head teacher. Think about what specific feedback you would need to get about:

- your letter of application
- your pre-interview visit
- your interview
- what you need to do to get the next job.

LOOKING FORWARD

This chapter has helped you bring together all the learning you have done through this book and throughout your course. It has helped you present the best picture of your skills and achievements to the people with whom you will be working in the next stage of your career.

Before you leave this book it is worth reflecting on the skills you will need for the next step you will take – your first teaching post. You will need to plan for:

- a smooth start to your new job

- a continuation of your learning and professional development.

Task 8: Starting Anew

- Think back to the start of your last period of teaching experience. Consult your log to remind yourself of what happened and how you felt:

    - what information did you need before you were able to start to teach your classes?
    - what did you need to find out about the expectations of the school, of the department and of the pupils, eg, were you expected to join a tutor group?
    - what did you need to know about the facilities and resources available to you?

- In your log, make a list of all the information you need to get from the school you are about to join. Figure 5.8 gives you an example of such a list.

- Check off all the information you have already received and think about how and when you are going to get the rest. You should plan to visit your new school and ask people for the information you require. You may need to arrange to spend several days at the school before term starts so that you can make your preparations.

You will undoubtedly feel that there is still a lot you need to learn about teaching; everyone feels like that. The DFE competences recognise that your initial training is only the start of your professional learning. The section on further professional development quoted earlier in this chapter gives an indication of some of the areas you will need to develop further.

Figure 5.8 *A new teacher's entitlement*

About my classes

- class lists
- schemes of work
- previous assessment records
- any special needs information
- a handover meeting with their previous teachers
- a meeting with their tutors or year heads
- my timetable

About expectations

- school year diary
- school curriculum policies
- school discipline policy
- staff handbook
- departmental policy on assessment
- a meeting with previous tutor of my tutor group
- a talk with the staff tutor
- an induction programme
- teaching load and policy on protection of non-contact time

About facilities and resources

- mark book
- a look at the room I will use
- access to stock/resource lists
- IT
- a mentor
- new teachers' groups in the school, in the area
- school plan/map
- map of the area

Task 9: Making the Most of the Induction Year

- Think about your teaching commitments in your new job and identify:
  - areas in which you know you will need support
  - areas in which you would welcome further development
  - the differences between your teaching experience to date and the demands of your new job.

- Anticipate how you would like your career to develop:
  - special expertise you would like to gain
  - other types of schools you would like to experience.

- Make a list in your log of sources of support and further professional development. Figure 5.9 offers some ideas.

- Discuss your list with another student teacher and with your mentors to make sure you have covered all your needs and all the possible sources of support.

- *Action plan* your further professional development
  - where and when is the support you need available?
  - who will you ask?
  - how will you ask for it?

Figure 5.9 *Sources of help and support*

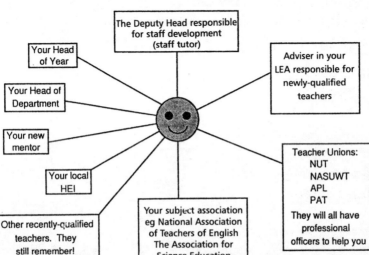

All there is left to do now is to make a start on your new job. Good luck!

The Competences

Your course has been designed to help you acquire and demonstrate specific competences. These are set down by the Department for Education in Circular 9/92, *Initial Teacher Training (Secondary)*, available from HMSO in London. It is against these competence statements that you will be assessed. You may find that your specific course offers a different version of this list of statements; it will, however, include all these key areas. (The numbered codes have been added by us for ease of reference throughout the text.)

SUBJECT KNOWLEDGE

Newly-qualified teachers should be able to demonstrate:

SK1 an understanding of the knowledge, concepts and skills of their specialist subjects and of the place of these subjects in the school curriculum;

SK2 knowledge and understanding of the National Curriculum attainment targets (NCATs) and the programmes of study (PoS) in the subjects they are preparing to teach, together with an under-standing of the framework of the statutory requirements;

SK3 a breadth and depth of subject knowledge extending beyond PoS and examination syllabuses in school.

SUBJECT APPLICATION

Newly-qualified teachers should be able to:

SA1 produce coherent lesson plans which take account of NCATs and of the school's curriculum policies;

SA2 ensure continuity and progression within and between classes and in subjects;

SA3 set appropriately demanding expectations for pupils;

SA4 employ a range of teaching strategies appropriate to the age, ability and attainment level of pupils;

SA5 present subject content in clear language and in a stimulating manner;

SA6 contribute to the development of pupils' language and communication skills;

SA7 demonstrate ability to select and use appropriate resources, including Information Technology.

CLASS MANAGEMENT

Newly-qualified teachers should be able to:

CM1 decide when teaching the whole class, groups, pairs, or individuals is appropriate for particular learning purposes;

CM2 create and maintain a purposeful and orderly environment for the pupils;

CM3 devise and use appropriate rewards and sanctions to maintain an effective learning environment;

CM4 maintain pupils' interest and motivation.

ASSESSMENT AND RECORDING OF PUPILS' PROGRESS

Newly-qualified teachers should be able to:

A&R1   identify the current level of attainment of individual pupils using NCATs, statements of attainment and end of key stage statements where applicable;

A&R2   judge how well each pupil performs against the standard expected of a pupil of that age;

A&R3   assess and record systematically the progress of individual pupils;

A&R4   use such assessment in their teaching;

A&R5   demonstrate that they understand the importance of reporting to their pupils on their progress and of marking their work regularly against agreed criteria.

FURTHER PROFESSIONAL DEVELOPMENT

Newly-qualified teachers should have acquired in initial training the necessary foundation to develop:

FPD1   an understanding of the school as an institution and its place within the community;

FPD2   a working knowledge of their pastoral, contractual, legal and administrative responsibilities as teachers;

FPD3   an ability to develop effective working relationships with professional colleagues and parents, and to develop their communication skills;

FPD4   an awareness of individual differences, including social, psychological, developmental and cultural dimensions;

FPD5   the ability to recognise diversity of talent including that of gifted pupils;

FPD6   the ability to identify special educational needs or learning difficulties;

FPD7   a self-critical approach to diagnosing and evaluating pupils' learning, including a recognition of the effects on that learning of teachers' expectations;

FPD8   a readiness to promote the moral and spiritual well-being of pupils.

APPENDIX 2

Tracking Your Progress

You will find it helpful to keep the competence statements in mind as you plan, record and gather evidence. Chapter 2 demonstrates how you might do this in terms of your experience of collaborative teaching. Chapter 4 gives you further guidance. You can use the same model as you progress through the book and through your course. It will be important to have regular review sessions and to use them to build your own map of your learning and to be aware of gaps you need to fill. We give here an example of the kind of grid you might develop to chart your progress.

Think about how to collect evidence of your increasing competence. Which documents will you use? Remember that you can use a single piece of evidence to demonstrate your competence in a number of areas. Your planning notes can show your competence in subject knowledge, subject application, class management and assessing and recording pupil progress. You will need to bring this evidence to meetings with your mentor.

DFE Competence Statements	Review Session 1	Review Session 2	Review Session 3	Review Session 4	Review Session 5
Subject Knowledge					
Subject Application					
Class Management					
Assessment and Recording of Pupils' Progress					
Further Professional Development					

APPNDIX

How Your Tasks will Help You to Acquire and Demonstrate Key Competences

DFE Competence Statements	Subject Knowledge	Subject Application	Class Management	Assessment and Recording of Pupils' Progress	Further Professional Development
Chapter 1					
Task 1					✓
Task 2					✓
Task 3					✓
Task 4		✓			✓
Task 5					✓
Task 6					✓
Task 7					✓
Task 8	✓	✓			
Task 9	✓	✓			✓
Task 10	✓				✓
Task 11	✓				✓

DFE Competence Statements	Subject Knowledge	Subject Application	Class Management	Assessment and Recording of Pupils' Progress	Further Professional Development
Chapter 2					
Task 1		✓			
Task 2	✓	✓		✓	
Task 3		✓		✓	✓
Task 4		✓			✓
Task 5		✓	✓	✓	
Task 6			✓	✓	✓
Chapter 3					
Task 1		✓			✓
Task 2	✓	✓	✓		
Task 3		✓	✓	✓	
Task 4		✓	✓	✓	✓
Task 5		✓	✓	✓	✓
Task 6	✓				✓
Task 7			✓		✓
Task 8					✓
Task 9	✓				✓
Task 10					✓
Chapter 4					
Task 1				✓	✓
Task 2		✓		✓	✓
Task 3		✓	✓	✓	
Task 4					✓
Task 5		✓		✓	
Task 6		✓		✓	✓
Task 7					✓
Chapter 5					
Task 1					✓
Task 2					✓
Task 3					✓
Task 4					✓
Task 5		✓			✓
Task 6					✓
Task 7					✓
Task 8		✓			✓
Task 9					✓